Chronicles From The Planet Business

An Eyewitness Account Of The Crimes, Passions,
Madness, And Downright Stupidity Of Modern Business

Barry J. Gibbons

CAPSTONE

First published 2000
Published simultaneously in the United States and the United Kingdom.

Capstone Publishing Limited
Oxford Centre for Innovation
Mill Street
Oxford OX2 0JX
United Kingdom
http://www.capstone.co.uk

Capstone Publishing Inc.
40 Commerce Park
Milford, CT 06460
USA
Contact: 203-878-6417

US Library of Congress Cataloging-in-Publication Data
A CIP catalog record for this book is available from the US Library of Congress

British Library Cataloguing in Publication Data
A CIP catalogue record for this book is available from the British Library

ISBN 1-84112-085-5

Designed and typeset by Kate Williams, Abergavenny
Printed and bound by Sheridan Books, Ann Arbor, Michigan

This book is printed on acid-free paper

Substantial discounts on bulk quantities of Capstone books are available to corporations, professional associations and other organizations. If you are in the USA or Canada, phone the LPC Group for details on (1-800-626-4330) or fax (1-800-243-0138). Everywhere else, phone Capstone Publishing on (+44-1865-798623) or fax (+44-1865-240941).

This book is in memory of Joss, our golden retriever, who died, at an age of nearly 15, in 1999.

In 30 years in business I have not met one human who had half his combined grace, honor, and dignity.

It makes you think …

These essays were originally published in the *Miami Herald*, and on their Website and on the Knight Ridder wire service. Most have been rewritten, some substantially. My thanks go to the *Herald's* long-suffering editorial team for welcome help along the way.

Introduction
What The HELL
Is This?

• •

• • • In 1997, I was into my fourth year of 'retirement' after leaving Big Business. It was my choice to retire. My bank managers (I seem to have acquired several) miss the old life (profoundly), but I do not. With Burger King's famed turnaround getting smaller in the rear-view mirror, I gave away my blue suit (the one with the elbows shining like Bette Davis's eyes) and began having *fun*.

I became involved in a gaggle of start-up companies on both sides of the Atlantic, and discovered, late in life, the terrors of burn-rate. By 1997, I was already drafting my second book, fired by the goal of giving it a longer title than the first. This I achieved. I also found myself entertaining business executives and customers from blue-chip companies across the world with my peculiar approach to keynote speaking.

But something was missing. Inspired by Richard Branson, I sought the satisfaction of achieving one of nature's last great challenges, and set off to be the first man to fly a hot-air balloon around Linda Tripp. But the Gods frowned, the winds were from the east, and it was not to be. Another challenge was needed.

After a two-year time-out, I decided to re-commence my bi-monthly business diary for the *Miami Herald* newspaper and Website. It was as though I'd never been away, and it was rapidly offered on the Knight Ridder newspaper group's wire service.

It became cult reading. I carelessly ended each column with my online address, and every week, without fail, an email would flood in—offering insurance.

Many thought I wrote for the simple pleasure of Monday-morning-quarterbacking the world of business, ripping into the many lunacies of modern commerce with my *Peter Drucker meets Aesop meets Monty Python* style of commentary. Many (who obviously don't know Jack about journalism) thought I did it for the money. They were all wrong.

My real goal was to chronicle the last years of the business millennium. No, really. I felt that posterity would appreciate an out-of-body look at a whole range of business issues as the world of commerce completed its last swirls before disappearing down the plug-hole of Y2K. A look, that is, as seen through the $\times 2$ magnification eyeglasses of someone who Tom Peters admiringly calls a madman—which remains my greatest, non-sexual compliment.

Very little in the world of business escapes my treatment. From my assorted world-wide vantage points, I thump my word processor, sometimes *wearing no clothes*, and let fly at a subject *du jour*. Business alliances, labor unions, the failings of capitalism, European unity, the death of the 'white-collar' job, cooking profits, business cultures, 'human' resource management, gaining from disaster, internationalism, and the fun of business travel are just a selection of the topics covered in this collection of 50 essays which cover most of the last two years of the millennium. There are tests for the intellect and good taste as, among other things, readers are introduced to the unlikely concept of *tosser-economies*.

I split my life between two domestic and business bases: one 40 miles north of London in the UK, one in Miami, Florida. Readers not only get a unique perspective of business from *both* sides of the Atlantic, they get to learn something of my life from my throwaway descriptions of my two very different, but parallel, existences. In England, the reader learns of my celebrated country home (with its Diana, Princess of Wales, Memorial Bedroom), guarded by my team of personal musket-bearing valets and a designer moat. In Miami, which I insist is 'near' America (and, like China, I believe, should be granted Most Favored Nation trading status with the US), the reader learns of the trials and tribulations of having to rely (almost every week) on the planet's biggest third-world airport. It is one of the few airports in the world, certainly in my experience, where the baggage-porters are trained to kill.

On behalf of the reader, I go on several business safaris—capturing images from the world of commerce in print from such unlikely vantage points as Russia, Southern Africa, and, yes, Tuscany. On one occasion, I even braved the gentle surf of Bermuda to bring the extra down-and-dirty authenticity that modern business book readers require.

I suspect, however, that it is the glimpses of the inner me that give this chronological collection *real* substance. Readers will learn of the happy childhood, playing with Czar Nicholas's children in his family's Summer Palace in St. Petersburg (Anastasia still emails me from her trailer park in Wisconsin). They will also learn of my time as a World War II ace fighter pilot. They will cheer the memory of me winning the 1917 Mixed Doubles Championships at Wimbledon, with a young Janet Reno. These events, however, will surprise many, particularly those who know (or think they know) my birth date to be 1946.

At various stages readers also learn of my weekly 'review' meetings with British Prime Ministers and my official mentor role with Prince William. This was the idea of his father (the Prince's, not mine) in an attempt to prepare William for a possible role in business *and* to throw a fire blanket over his exploding hormones (the Prince's, not mine). The reader will learn of my PR consultancy with Saddam Hussein. Glimpses are given of my search for inner peace (or my 'tin of peaches' as my long-ago chauffeur used to call it), with my regular retreats into the wild hills of Wales (eating only small mountain lions previously thought to be extinct). My unparalleled commitment to a cause is also revealed. Which other Captain of Industry would support a product launch (Burger King's BK Broiler) by tracing one of the routes of the Crusades, on foot, and lighting a small, unbleached candle in each chapel on the way? I also reveal my teenage formula for winning girlfriends, which involved copious amounts Brylcreem (in my hair), copious amounts of beer (in my stomach, heading for my bladder), and dancing as though I was in the advanced stages of Parkinson's Disease. This formula *never once succeeded*.

My aim has been to provide an eyewitness account of business in our time. A collection of essays that is riotous, but thoughtful; bizarre but savvy; manic, but balanced. It is corner-stoned by my own real, hard, measurable business success, but unafraid to theorize. Sometimes it is, and does, *all of these things at once*—sometimes in one sentence. Punctuation was never my strong point.

There is something in it for *everybody* who has experienced business, of any kind or at any level, or who plans to do so soon. There are ideas to make the Chairman of the Board look thoughtfully out of the window of the private jet. There are tools for the thousands (millions) of ordinary employees to use; those who offer up a third of their lives in sacrifice to the alter of enterprise and commerce at *all* levels. There are just plain laughs for those who need a break.

It is a unique look at the closing years of the *first* millennium of business as we know it. Or as we *thought* we knew it.

Barry Gibbons
Bedford, England & Miami,USA
November 1999
email: GibbonFile@aol.com

1997

August 25th
LoveThine Enemy.com

• •

• • • Around 825BC, on one of those cold, clear Mediterranean mornings (the kind where you are fooled into going for an early morning swim, and then find, if you are a male of the species, that you need your wife's eyebrow tweezers to wee wee), the inhabitants of the city of Troy were woken by loud yelling. Rubbing the sleep from their eyes, they stumbled up the city wall ramparts to see what all the fuss was about. Peering over the top, they saw a *humungous* wooden horse.

Contrary to legend, their initial response was not to cry out 'What, in the name of Clinton's Trouser Zip, is *that*?' because it was self-evident it was a big horse made of timber. No, their general response was '*Why*, in the name of O.J.Simpson.Dot.Backslash.Dot.

Backslash.Dot.Com, is it there?' History, of course, has informed us of the reason, just as it revealed it to them a couple of nights later.

Something very similar must have occurred at the 1997 Apple Convention. Steve Jobs (the computer industry's Harrison Ford) was giving his keynote address to the beleaguered Appleites when he suddenly flipped a switch and introduced a giant, live, satellite-link picture of their new partner-in-recovery-to-be: *It was Bill Gates*. He was in on the conspiracy, and—would you believe—smirking.

Aaarrggh! Apple's arch enemy, their nemesis, their Darth Vader—all rolled into one—appearing on their parade! Previously, Apple's official position on Bill Gates had been to lobby for legislation that would prohibit him from breeding. But worse, much worse, was to come. He had, apparently, scoured the back of his couch for some loose change and bought $150 million worth of Apple's stock and, to cap it all, promised some joint software development programs between Microsoft and Apple. Grown Appleites cried, and many of their code writers (sitting in the cheap seats upstairs) threw up over the balcony. They saw their own version of the wooden horse—and it was already inside the city walls.

Turns out they should not have looked on Uncle Bill with such mistrust.

I know Gates well of course—for the past few years we've jousted amicably about who would be the world's highest net worth individual whenever *Fortune* magazine next printed the list. It's fair to say that he's recently pulled away in the race—as he approached and then passed the $50 billion mark. I, of course, have been handicapped by having two sons living and studying in England, which incurs an annual net worth *reduction* of $7 billion). But the silver medal is fine by me, and we remain firm friends. I can only see altruism and philanthropy in his motives with Apple, and personally pooh-pooh the cynics who say that it is driven by darker goals.

What may surprise both my loyal readers is my belief, then and now, that this move made a lot of sense for Apple — and I raise my hat to Jobs for his vision and courage. These two attributes were, of course, missing by the bucketful in Apple's departed CEO, who's name will be forgotten by history in just a few moments longer than it took me to forget it.[1]

Strategic alliances can make big sense today—particularly when you're down on your luck and you need to change big things quickly. This move makes sense for Apple for two reasons:

- Apple's unique operating system, beloved by its *aficionados* and nobody else, has had its 15 minutes of fame and is now being swamped. Unless you're a real specialist and/or attempting to be the first graphic Van Gogh, you'd be mad not to invest in some PC 'Wintel' combo.

- At a stroke, however, this move made Apple's future and positioning look different—aka better—from every vantage point (employee, investor and consumer). Was *that* ever needed at the time.

Strategic alliances can make big sense today—particularly when you're down on your luck and you need to change big things quickly

In 1989 Burger King was nearly dead in the water. There were some things we could do to start the healing process—such as fix our supply chain and run our restaurants better—but it was a difficult task to convince the American nation that we were no longer just about blue-collar Bubba but a valid family-friendly dining offering. So, we developed our Kid's Club, and lighter meals for mom and the kids—but the real breakthrough came when we agreed strategic marketing alliances with Disney and Coca-Cola. At a stroke (well … as near as you can get with a mighty sized juggernaut) we looked different from every vantage point and, as Disney and Coca-Cola benefited significantly from the alliances, we all looked back on a win-win game plan.

Strategic alliances are a valid way to develop your business today. They can work for businesses of all shapes and sizes (even start-ups), and don't necessarily have to involve equity positions. If you are thinking of expanding internationally, it is almost impossible to

---

1. You know who I mean. Him. Whatsit … has a G in his name somewhere. Thingy. He wrote a book … C'mon, *one* of us must remember …

enter some markets without such a partner—Japan being a classic example. Try it sometime if you don't believe me.

The globalization of business and the erosion of trade barriers have seen the growth of strategic alliances in many previously insular industries—notably automobiles and aircraft manufacture. It's going to be perfectly feasible to have your investor base in one country, production in another, and your market in others. You might well have stakeholders and alliances in all of the above.

In this game, sometimes you are required to look on an old enemy as a potential friend, and that's always tough. Letting Bill Gates into bed with you, *whoever* you are, can be pretty scary. But it might be just the thing to change your market from a zero-sum game, where one party can only win at the expense of the other. And, what is more, it might enable you to do this legally, which always helps.

But it isn't always the right thing to do. So here's a piece of practical advice for you: if you look over your own particular city walls, and the wooden horse (or the satellite link, or whatever) you see standing there looks anything like a big wooden Al Dunlap (a man who, for years, suffered from delusions of adequacy) do not arrange for a feasibility study, or seek the advice of consultants, or instigate a six-month option analysis. Go right downstairs and burn it. And then still run like hell back into the mountains.

September 8th
Soft Porn And The Labor Movement

• •

• • • Back in the 1970s, I took up my first management position in the beer business in England. Part of my new empire was a distribution depot, where trucks would be loaded with full kegs of beer and would be out delivering to bars before the first sparrow had passed wind in the morning (about 6:15 a.m.).

On my first day, I got there early—still only just in time to see the last loads leave the yard. These were trucks driven by *draymen*, a name reflecting a time when the vehicles were pulled by dray horses. These guys were traditionally unionized, and aggressively so. In this case, the shop steward was a card carrying Communist, and saw our depot as one of the great theaters of the Struggle against Management, the Bourgeoisie, and (I think) his mother-in-law.

The required management skills to handle all this needed to blend locker-room dick-headed confrontationalism with the sensitivity of a child psychologist. Here beganneth my first lesson.

The management skills need to blend locker-room dick-headed confrontationalism with the sensitivity of a child psychologist

On the morning in question, I joined my shift supervisor in his tiny office, and inquired if all was well in his world. He replied that it was, and that the morning had passed without incident. But then he remembered there had been a spot of bother with Harry (one of our more militant drivers). He'd had to give him a *formal oral*.

Now, I ask you to remember this was the 1970s and, although nobody had yet heard of Monica Lewinsky and her re-patterned dress, we were not *that* sheltered. I was in my early thirties, and it will not surprise you that about a thousand different images flashed through my mind. Few of them would survive a PG13 rating.

It transpired, however, that a formal oral was a form of disciplinary warning, and the second stage in the appropriate procedure agreed with the labor union. It followed an informal oral, and was succeeded by an informal, then formal *written* warning and then right through to (I presume) an informal public beheading. A similar procedure existed for when the boot was on the other foot, and the union wanted to raise a grievance with management.

The ritual fire-dance that is the relationship between management and unions has contributed to a profoundly entertaining adult life for me. Watching *both* sides claiming victory after a long drawn out pissing contest (such as that which ripped UPS apart in 1997), when in reality both have lost irredeemable ground, is like watching two bald guys argue over a comb. They should put this stuff on the stage.

I'll surprise some of you by confessing admiration and support for the appropriate organization of labor, and its role in developing the *balance* of our civilization has been obvious. In the early nineteenth century, in the cotton mills of the industrial north of England, a confused and startled workforce saw machines being introduced that replaced 10, then 100, spinners; so, at night, they broke into the factories and destroyed them in a misguided attempt to defend their jobs, communities, and way of life . It eventually took 12,000 English troops to smash what became the Luddite movement, and, nearly two centuries later, it is hard for me not to warm to the nobility of their cause. Had I lived then, I am sure I would have been with them, just as I'm sure I would have proudly fought against many of the atrocities of industrialization.

The de-humanization of men, women, and children in pursuit of the three Ps (profit, productivity, and progress) has pockmarked the face of business development in the west during the past 200 years, and many, many such challenges still exist in countries going through their own industrial adolescence. There is still much for organized labor to fight for.

I guess the spectacle is diminishing, although in the US the recent baseball strike illustrated both the glories and the idiocies of the great struggle. I also guess, today, that if you have a grievance against your employer, it makes more and more sense to by-pass the union representatives and their cumbersome grievance procedures—much better to call your attorney and sue the SOBs for millions.

The strike weapon is a bit like smallpox— it still exists, but it is far from the threat it was

If there is a collective grievance, and the union want to take it to the limit, the strike weapon is a bit like smallpox—it still exists, but it is far from the threat it was. Determined management (for the wrong or right reasons) can now take and hold a hard line. Public sympathy is usually important in securing a 'win' for labor, and it is tough to get when you are disrupting people's lives for a cause that has moved from fighting for a living wage or civilized working conditions to stock option schemes, pension funds, and the defense of indolence.

Labor does need to organize in post-industrial society, but its role needs to move from processing individual disciplinary issues and grievances. It also needs to move away from targeted collective confrontation. Strangely enough, it can find the genesis of its new role back with the Luddites.

There are new forces at work today that threaten postindustrial society in the same way that the new spinning machines threatened life in the early mill towns. Globalization has meant that labor can be sourced from anywhere in the world where it is available at the lowest price. In addition, there are high *indirect* costs of labor associated with full-time employment, which are leading to much outsourcing and part time employment in the hope of avoiding them. As ever, the unenlightened companies will get it wrong; the enlightened ones will get the balance right.

Just as stockholders and consumers have become more vigilant in looking after their interests, so must labor. But the key theater for this battle must be the boardroom, not the machine room, and the challenge is one of *influence,* not confrontation. We will now live forever in a world of deregulated, free, markets, and the best corporate strategies will be determined by enlightened self-interest. The challenge for labor is to recognize and reflect its role as an *investing stakeholder* in the company, and get its point of view on the boardroom table so that the right decisions can be taken for the right reasons.

It will, sadly, mean fewer *formal orals.* For different reasons, Bill Clinton and I will mourn their passing.

September 22nd
BIGMACATTACK!

• •

• • • I am delighted with Burger King's continued renaissance. For five years I was on their team sheet, and for the past few have cheered them lustily from the cheap seats in the grandstand.

I am both proud and delighted to acknowledge that my management team began the great fight-back in the early 1990s. We worked hard, and did a lot of things. Some franchisees were against what we were trying to change, and how we were trying to change it. That is putting it politely, but with the benefit of hindsight the death threats were quite entertaining. Some, however, were in favor, and everybody managed to contribute in some way. Gradually the old boat swung around, and headed for calmer water.

If you want the full truth, however, there was another factor that worked in our favor. For five glorious years (at least they were from *my* vantage point), our 'arch' (deliberate pun intended) rival peed on their own shoes with astonishing regularity. In fact, they neatly broke all three of the Commandments which rule fast food retailing:

- Thou shalt not market a new product (Arch Deluxe) by alienating your existing core customers, with an advertising campaign designed to deliberately 'belittle' children.

- Thou shalt not offer a hamburger with seaweed anywhere near it (the McLean).

- Thou shalt not offer a product that looks like a part which broke off the MIR space station (McRib).

The McManager in charge of that lot is now probably running snake control in Ireland, so it came as a shock that Burger King's 1997 main market initiative was built around the launch of a new hamburger called the Big King. We were told initial sales were good, but all that tells us is that Americans will try anything once, a proposition proved by the existence of hominy grits. Then it all went quiet.

I'm sure the new product will have been researched, but so was New Coke. For the latter (as I understand it), 4.7 billion people were asked if they would buy New Coke. Of those, 97.38% ticked the box marked 'very probably.' Later, when asked why they didn't, they ticked the box marked 'Well, I changed my mind. So sue me.'

As I have often preached, the key to branding is *distinction,* and there is still no better one word definition of the concept. It is not about relative price or quality, but how distinct the product or service is in the clutter of its market place. Thanks to the vision of founders Jim Mclemore and Dave Egerton, Burger King has strong market distinction, and not just for its main brand name. Below it are brands that are major international players in their own right: Kid's Club, BK Broiler ... and a huge one called The Whopper. Burger King sells over 2 million Whoppers alone, *every day*.

So, why put a new brand in your own portfolio, that needs a ton of money to launch and maintain, and position it as a me-too against the Big Mac—and even use 'Big' in the name? For every gain made at the expense of the Big Mac, *it will make another at the expense of the Whopper—damaging the home team's brand equity.*

In my observation, the best brand managers on earth are Coca-Cola, and the lessons from their continued success (and occasional failures and rapid recoveries) are there for all to see. Work at keeping your brand(s) relevant and distinct. If there is room for another clone in the core market, try and *add* to your own brand equity (e.g. Diet Coke), not somebody else's. Can you imagine Coca-Cola launching Tepsi-Cola?

The Whopper itself has the Double Whopper and Whopper Junior, both of which could be built in a way which confirms market distinction *and* strengthens the Whopper's equity.

New product launches, however well researched, are a crapshoot

Of course, this is just my view. As Dennis Miller, the ascerbic American comedian would put it, 'I could be wrong'. I hope I am. New product launches, however well researched, are a crapshoot. Personally, I find the best way to minimize the risk is to digest all the data, make your decision, and then sacrifice a small mammal. For a big launch I do something really special. I remember, for the high profile launch of the BK Broiler, walking across Southern Europe tracing the route of the first Crusades. I lit a small, unbleached candle in each church on the way.

I wish the Big King well, despite my reservations. As we are all headed inexorably towards a federally mandated diet of alfalfa sprouts and milk treated with our own urine, it is important that there are some products left that bring a smile to the face of Dr. Kervorkian.

October 6th
Decision Time?
Try Winging It

• •

• • • The death of Mother Theresa—surely the greatest nonfiction role model of all time—has put further pressures on the sluggish canonization processes of the Catholic Church, which is already under fire from the worldwide public groundswell demanding saint-hood for two people while they are still alive (namely Hillary Rodham Clinton and Richard Branson). The events in Calcutta have sim-ply highlighted the ossified decision making mechanisms of the Vatican. Remember, it was only in this decade that they ratified the findings of Copernicus (1473–1543).

Business, however, should resist the temptation to be smug. The sad fact is that it still mirrors much of the Church's aversion to taking speedy decisions, despite having access to more information (and more information *faster*) that at any time in history.

A while back, I was in Europe working with an organization that brought together, in the loosest possible sense, a collection of individual accounting firms outside the Big Six. There was a real opportunity (which was probably better defined as a real *need*) for them to work together across international boundaries to compete with the giants.

I confess I have never been at ease with the accountancy profession, or accountants. My academic failings in the subject are nothing short of legendary, and my suspicion is that most would-be accountants, immediately after their actual birth, probably went back in to check that all the lights were switched off. Even to my uneducated and cynical mind, however, the areas of potential synergy for these guys were significant. Even without considering partnerships or joint ventures, a range of simple activities such as networking, introductions, database sharing and common systems development would help them compete for the business of true international clients.

They had seen the possibilities. Which was the end of the good news. This is how they had gone about making them happen: two years previously they had started the debate on who should be on the committee to think about it all. No real progress had been made. It was agreed at our meeting that a formal *nominating* committee would now take over, taking a *year* to consider who should be on the working party. This body would then, in turn, go away and look at the actual problems and opportunities. The time scale envisaged for this process? Between one and three years. Then, of course, a mechanism would have to be designed to take actual decisions, which, I suspect, would be under the chairmanship of Spock, the Vulcan, as the likely timing of this step would take it into Star Date territory.

We talk a lot about the pace of change in business, and much of it is a crock

We talk a lot about the pace of change in business, and much of it is a crock. Sometimes, all the talk itself puts back-pressure on the speed of our decision making processes. There is an irony here. We now have almost *infinite* databases available via data-carrying phone lines. We have *huge* analytical firepower available at a power point on a desk. Both, however, can combine to *elongate* decisions because we can research the options endlessly.

We live in a world where every fundamental of every business is capable of structural change within the timeframe of what used to be the business planning cycle; between three and five years. The days of spending a gazillion dollars on consultants, and preparing a traditional business plan, with loads of nice graphics in the appendices, must end. The paradox is that the more we have the ability to analyze and research, the more pragmatism may have to play a part.

It has long been my view that you can get into a position where you can be about 80% sure of a decision in any walk of life, including business. It is also my observation that you can then spend another two years moving that degree of certainty to about 82%. My instinct tells me (and you) to take the decision at the 80% point, get the boat away from the pier, and then fix it as you go. If the practical experience proves you were wrong, it is unlikely that the extra two years of desktop research would have revealed the fault line in your thinking. If you do end up in the swamp, I suggest you definitely adapt this approach to decision making to get out of it.

The paradox is that the more we have the ability to analyze and research, the more pragmatism may have to play a part

I've not finished yet; saving the best till last. If you have a *big* decision facing your business (let's say something more substantive than allowing the employees to wear polo shirts on Fridays), get the required people in a room, away from their normal workplaces, give them the appropriate summary information, and tell them *they won't eat or drink* until a decision is recorded. A couple of further actions help this process: take the chairs and phones out of the room; and add a rider—if anybody's mobile goes off, they will be fired. This whole, short, alien process will bring astonishing results. Trust me.

I have strayed from the subject of sainthood. I want you to know that I have decided to veto the proposal that Prince Charles should get one. I simply can't just hand one to a man who has a full six-pack, but clearly lacks the plastic thing to hold it together. I know he looks very worthy, particularly when he wears his kilt, but I fear there may be character defects above and beyond those normally associated with his lineage. How else do you explain the fact that, after every occasion that he has been to our house for luncheon, I have this urge to count the silver flatware?

October 20th
Come Fly
With Me

• •

• • • Great song title; great lyric. If it had been written today, of course, it would need changing. It would have to be 'Come fly with me—but please check in at least two hours in advance and you can only have one carry-on bag.'

Few know of my exploits as a World War II fighter pilot. But when you think about it, it is not really surprising that combat-hardened veterans like myself became Captains of Industry. Moving at warp speed is second nature, and getting things done against strong resistance (such as G-force, diversity workshops, and so on) is all part of a day's work.

The story of my airborne heroism was, of course, told in my best-selling autobiography (*Gibbons Flies Undone 1939–45*), and it is a pity more of my breed have not emerged to inspire and direct industry—in particular the confused world of commercial air traffic itself.

There is a whole range of odd stuff going on. Strategic alliances are on, then off. In the (deregulated) US, stripped-bare cut-pricers are forcing the majors into response programs that overtly threaten service and covertly threaten safety. The FAA is unsure whether its role is to prevent, or react to, disaster. In (regulated) Europe, where less than 10% of routes have a choice of airline, all but the peanut vendors are staring at imminent deregulation in open terror.

I had the recent qualified delight of visiting the old Soviet Union, where some of the wonders of the world sit side by side with its miseries. That paradox was appropriate, for we were gathered for an international seminar on the airline industry.

As it started, I thought I'd been smoking something illegal. I listened in amazement to the industry spending the first day *congratulating* itself. Job well done … blah-blah-blah … however, can't be complacent … blah-blah … customers statistically satisfied … future bright… blah-blah … business to double in next 15 years …treble in 20 years … blah-blah-blah …

Whoa, guys! Pass the sick bag! As a massive user of airline and airport services, let me bring you in on a little secret: *you suck*. You have massive repeat usage by customers, but that does not come through loyalty or respect. It comes because you are the only act in town (now known as the America Online syndrome).

The airline industry is now the labor pain in the birth process of reaching a destination

Unlike the Orient Express or a sea cruise liner, nobody goes anywhere to actually fly; it is a means to an end. In my eyes the airline industry is now the labor pain in the birth process of reaching a destination, and my distant and peripheral memories of labor pain are that it falls on a spectrum ranging from a couple of hours' discomfort to double digit hours of hell on earth. Unless you are prepared to pay thousands of dollars for a first class fare—which, on an overnight flight, buys you a 'bed' you would reject outright in a $30 a night motel—the total package has become a joke.

Either side of the time you spend with the user-unfriendly airline, of course, you are at the mercy of the airport service teams. These top and tail your in-flight misery with special treats of their own ('er ... sorry folks ... it appears there's a plane already occupying our gate ... we'll just have to park over here for a while ... *please don't stand up* ... sorry about your connections ... I'm sure we'll have more information in a while ... *please do not stand up ...*').

I use many airports, but my own beloved Miami ranks in the top five on the planet for sustained traveler-battering. In about 10–20 years, the world will have a fourth financial and cultural epicenter to add to Tokyo, New York/Washington, and London. The Hispanic world will deservedly shape and define its own, and it ought to be Miami, but it won't be. High on the list of the reasons why it won't be is that international business people view a trip through the Miami immigration and customs processes with the same enthusiasm as root canal surgery.

The whole flying experience can, and should, be different. Breakthrough speed increases and longer haul flights mean the agony can be profoundly cut in duration, which, I guess, would be everybody's number one plea. New technology means planes with 650–700 passenger carrying potential will be with us within five years, which would enable a radical reform of traditional in-flight seating and service. Do we have to get on and off through just one door? Technology already exists to completely re-think the galley/trolley-catering shambles, which hasn't been structurally changed in decades. There is simply no need for immigration processes to be reminiscent of Ellis Island, certainly for short business or leisure visits. Most of that could be done at the airport of embarkation—or even during the flight—on heavily trafficked routes. And are we sure there is no alternative to the Miami-style zoo for luggage reclaim, which is followed by exposure to luggage porters who would intimidate Mike Tyson?

The opportunity exists *now* to redefine the whole experience. By the year 2001 flying could be worth doing in its own right, but it

I've seen the industry in action, and it is an intoxicating mix of humbug and lethargy

will not happen. I've seen the industry in action, and it is an intoxicating mix of humbug and lethargy. The industry doesn't believe it's broken, so why should it mend it? And we, the users, simply have no leverage.

My immediate action plan is to do two things in response to all this. First, I'm buying stock in companies that supply peanuts in Europe, and, second, on account of the panning I've given Miami Airport in these few well-chosen words I'm switching to Fort Lauderdale airport till it cools down here a bit. Or I can grow a serious beard.

Put That Bomb Down. Trust The Market

• •

• • • *St. Petersburg, Russia:* It is hard not to cry as I chew on my early evening pickled garlic, stare out over the gray waters towards Finland, and remember my childhood here. We had a small summer palace, and happy times with our neighbors, the Romanov family. It ended so sadly.

Tragedy struck, of course, in 1918 when this delightful family was butchered in the infamous cellar at Ekaterinburg. All, that is, but the delightful Anastasia—Ana to her friends—who miraculously survived and still emails me to this day from her home in a trailer park in Wisconsin. My family escaped with a suitcase full of our larger jewels, and watched with horror as the dark curtain of totalitarianism came down on this fine land for more than 70 years.

In the early 1990s it was suddenly, and unexpectedly, lifted again. We celebrated and looked forward to all Russians rapidly playing catch-up with the west on the back of capitalism. We figured the uninhibited application of the free market laws—the 'invisible' hand, prices set by the unfettered meeting of supply and demand, the unrestricted mobility of labor, capital, and resources (and so on)—would kick in and everybody would win. These poor folks, whose noses had been pressed against the glass for decades, would soon have two cars, cellular phones, Direct TV, beepers, and 16 credit cards each. Some would have bumper stickers telling the world their child was an honor student.

What fools we were. A decade later the position has worsened for most Russians. There are no new jobs, houses, or services for Ivan and Svetlana Public. They are a couple of bad harvests away from hyper-inflation. Crime and drunkenness are rampant. There are no more pets around the apartments; they have long gone into the infamous 'hunting sausages' that now form a staple part of the local diet. Huge snakes and rodents—many of them 70 feet long— roam the streets. It is now socially acceptable for families to eat their weakest children on the feast day of St. Isaac.

What the hell went wrong? Why is capitalism failing these people? The only real change it has brought is to add uncertainty to already dreary lives. The people are confused, angry, frustrated, and jealous. And the *really* bad news is that a couple of hundred nuclear bombs have gone missing.

The reality is that there is no such thing as a true free market today We are forced to face two facts. First, the reality is that *there is no such thing as a true free market* today. Even the most *laissez-faire* of western governments still account for between a quarter and a half of their nation's spending, and they are notoriously ineffective and inefficient in so doing. In Russia there is then a sinister additional factor; 40% of gross domestic product is estimated to pass through the hands of organized crime. These folk have their own goals, and they are not usually to do with the well being of the population as a whole. If you then figure that the bulk of what's left is in the hands of multinational corporations—often taking decisions outside the country for the benefit of non-Russian investors—you begin to see the futility of the 'invisible hand' of Adam Smith's free market creating new wealth for every Russian.

While we are at it, lets face another unpalatable fact about capitalism. Even if there was a free market, the history of capitalism shows *it does not benefit the poor in the short term*; in fact it is much easier to prove the opposite. The reality is that capitalism is *not* about the redistribution of wealth, and, if it were, it is towards the already wealthy and the investor in its early years. Don't get me wrong here— it's the best system there is over the long haul—but that can take decades, or even centuries. On the journey, capitalism is often an unattractive mix of rich people in poor countries and poor people in rich countries.

My hands are now too cold to write anymore, so I head for my humble dwelling (Grand Europe Hotel, St. Petersburg, $400 per night, mini bar and *masseuse* extra). A disheveled man approaches me selling black market Beluga Caviar. The (dollar) price is simply too good to resist so I buy a kilo, knowing that I am sadly adding to the whole shambolic *mal du siecle*.

Ana will be angry with me when she hears about this. So she should be. I will expect a bitter email.

November 17th
Vive La Différence! Vive La EOC!

• •

• • • *Chantilly, Northern France:* A few of us gather to celebrate the French government's latest idiocy: the introduction of the 35 hour working week. We decide to roast one of the small wild boar that roam the local woodlands. It was unfortunately run over by one of the three French truck drivers opting to work this month, and who zoom noisily up and down the once busy road that heads down to the capital.

Waiting for dinner, we ponder the age-old question: has there ever been a bigger gap between the attraction of a country, and those that populate it? This is a nation, remember, that insists there is a distinction between Napoleon and Hitler, and which continually elects odious, interfering, misdirected governments.

'French planning'—i.e. putting the state at the heart of the decision making process—can be traced back to the seventeenth century. It prospered under Gaullism and the nationalization programs of Mitterand, and thrives today. It is the opposite of everything we are, and stand for, in the US and UK—correct?

Yeah, right. We're really no different over here. In fact, we may be worse, because much of the dumb intervention we suffer comes in indirect ways. Under Clinton's Reign of Terror, the trustbusters of the American Justice department decided that Microsoft had become too big and successful, and at one stage whacked a $1 million a day fine on it, before commencing litigation that should clear up well before the end of the *next* millennium. The crime? Bundling up its Internet browser with its operating system. I understand Bill Gates paid the fine on his AAdvantage Visa to get the air miles. Sure, Microsoft is big and successful, but so are Coca-Cola, McDonald's, Intel, General Electric, Ford, and maybe 100 others. In the crazy paced world of computer software and cyberspace it actually *helps* all of us in the west, given that our standard of living is a direct function of our competitiveness at home and abroad, that we have a giant prepared to fund the outrageous research and development costs, and give us one operating system. Remember what happened with the dual system video wars a while back?

Somebody has decided, however, that Microsoft's browser doesn't have *real* competition, but is it their fault that the other wannabes are under-resourced and inept? Poor dears. Mrs. Reno, who demonstrates an astonishing consistency in picking the wrong dead horse to flog, added another one to her impressive list of snafus. Don't fix something till it's broke, ma'am.

This interference crap doesn't just play out at national level for big brands—it can hit anywhere, any time, anybody

This interference crap doesn't just play out at national level for big brands. It can hit anywhere, any time, anybody. In 1992, Burger King's headquarters was all but destroyed by

Hurricane Andrew, and needed such a rebuild it was classified (locally) as a new building under the Americans With Disabilities Act. I had no problem with the principle, but exercised my presidential line item veto when I saw one proposed change: the provision of a handicapped parking space for a hugely overweight male employee. This was not a disabled employee. This was a *Big Fat Bastard.* I saw this as an insult to the genuinely disabled, who have my utmost admiration as they battle through life with a hand of cards dealt them while their God was on his lunch break. I eventually won, using the logic that it would actually serve this guy well to have a parking space at the *other end* of the lot; the walk might get some oxygen pumping through the cholesterol. But how many other such 'interpretive' nonsenses are now *intervening* in local business life? They come at you from all angles, at all levels. No business, or even part of it, is left untouched.

Miami's famous 'Joe's' Stone Crab restaurant brings us one of the most bilious examples of recent times. In 1997 and 1998, the Equal Employment Opportunity Commission, unaided by any actual individuals filing a charge, filed discrimination complaints against the restaurant for not hiring 'enough' women. 'Enough' was defined as being *in line with the local population percentage*! Eventually the court found Joe's guilty of unintentional discrimination, winning the Annual Oxymoron Award outright. Then *Monty Python* took over the script, and court appointees actually *took part in the ensuing interview processes for waiting-on staff.* So here we have the public sector telling a company in the private sector whom to hire, not on the basis of how good they are, or with any commercial dimension in mind, but on the basis of their genital appendage (or lack of same). The net result of this abomination, that probably had the Founding Fathers spinning merrily in their graves? *Fewer females actually applied for the job* than would normally have been the case. And the taxpayer spent a bundle of dumb money. Whoop, as they say, pee.

Do you spot the irony here? The baby boomers now in charge are the group that gave us protest, draft-dodging, free love, instant divorce, and the drug culture. But *never* has a generation been more interventionist, meddling, and nannying once it got the keys to the executive toilet. Of course, it is well meant, and some of it needed, but what the hell happened to the litmus paper test of

common sense? We now have communities introducing legal curfews
for children, which gets them off the
street at a certain hour at night. The
'policing' for the rank interference in personal liberty *and*
responsibility? The taxpayer. Again-o. I read recently of a Californian
surfer who is (quite rightly in my view) suing a fellow surfer for
stealing his wave. Well, that I find hilarious and totally justified.
Creative litigation. America at its best. It's the other interventionist,
interfering stuff that's scary.

N*ever* has a generation been more interventionist, meddling, and nannying

Back on the terrace of my Chantilly *auberge*, I choose a heady
1961 Chateau St Julien claret to accompany my wild boar road-
kill. We follow with a simple *tarte au tatin,* which I wash down
with a divine young Muscat de Baumes-de-Venise. I dream of *des
papillions* on Provence meadows. *Vive la France!* Hasn't that always
been my position?

December 1st

El Niño And Storms In The Workplace

• •

• • • The effects of *El Niño* are far-reaching. I hear of a lawsuit brought by the flight attendants of one of America's great airlines, which shall remain nameless, save to say it's initials are *very* near the start of the alphabet. They are seeking punitive damages for the suffering caused by their exposure to *passive smiling*. They, themselves, of course, stopped smiling about three years ago as a result of a Federal Aviation Directive (or FAD, as it's known), but claim they are now being affected by passengers who smile at random, *without a thought about the risk this could bring to others*. I put all this, and much more, down to the warming of the ocean.

I have also been blaming *El Niño* for the recent whining noise in the atmosphere. On further investigation, however, I find it to be the sound emitted by the male middle management and staff of America and Britain. They are largely white (like their collars), and are reeling from another round of lay-offs such as those announced by Kodak, Levi Strauss, Woolworth, IBM and AT&T. There have been 35 million of these lay-offs in the past couple of decades, and there's no real sign of a slow down.

I have long argued that mass firings (can we stop calling this 're-engineering' please?) are often misdirected and almost always managed appallingly. You cannot just cut your way to success: the trick in business is to constantly strive to do *more* of *better* with *less*, not less of worse with less. But, one way or another, *less* is a fact of life for the white-collar tribe, and it will get far, *f-a-r*, worse before it gets better.

The trick in business is to constantly strive to do more of better with less, not less of worse with less

The moaning has reached deafening levels, and I'm sick of it. Does anybody know a reason why this bunch of losers should have special protection? Nobody protected the cotton workers when the spinning jenny arrived, and autoworkers went the way of the buffalo when the robots landed. There has always been collateral damage (as the Pentagon sensitively calls it) with progress of any kind, and the affected species has to regroup and reinvent itself, or go the way of the Dodo.

Who are these folk anyway, and just what are these jobs that are disappearing ? I was on a TV business panel recently and a guy phoned in asking what percentage did we think the average white-collar worker gave of his/her personal *potential* ability and resource to the job? He thought it could be as low as 50%. The three of us looked at each other and doubted it was as *high* as 15%. Is that really worth defending?

I have a theory, unsullied by any deep research. If you send every current white-collar worker out of the office into the yard, and only let back in those that have a stretched and flexible job description, *and* who are then armed with the *latest* technology and software, you would re-employ only about 50% of them. Now bite on this bullet: within 20 years, in my view, *another* 47% will be redundant. Add that up for my 2020 vision: only *three* out of every 100 current white-collar jobs will remain, and I think I'm optimistic. Nobody (I repeat, *nobody*) starting work today will complete 40 years' service with one organization, and the vast, vast majority will never do more than 5–10 years.

Ironically, the forecast chaos contains the seeds of some *very* positive things. The great inhibitor to genuine delegation and empowerment is the reluctance by those receiving the 'honor' to do anything with it. Folk dare not take risks, and they are scared to stand out in the crowd, or use their initiative, because they are worried about the security of their jobs if anything goes wrong. Well, the good news is *you're gonna lose your job anyway,* so let it rip, make a statement, fulfill yourself and make your job worthwhile, instead of turning up for the living death that currently eats up a third of your life. Amazingly you will probably thrive, and be one of the three who survive. That is, if you *want* to survive, because if you start behaving like this you'll soon be off to something better.

I have long believed that if God existed (or exists), She was a woman. My reasoning is simple: if God was/is a 'He,' those dangly things we have around our groins would *not* have been on the outside. As a longtime amateur soccer player, you may trust me on this. But there are other reasons why we should question Deity's conventionally accepted gender. You see, women have already got this complex aspect of the business challenge figured out. Somehow. And they have it figured out so well, they must have had inside knowledge. Big business has done them no favors either (for entirely different reasons), so they've *abandoned it,* and the most vibrant sector of the economy is now that of small businesses owned and/ or run by women. Ironically they are mopping up all the opportunities created by downsizing and outsourcing. *Catch on* and *catch up,* guys.

Me? I've already done it. I work for a company who's notepaper heading spells half my old school motto. I have a fixed and committed overhead (or burn rate, as we entrepreneurs call it) of precisely zero. Now I'm off to catch a plane. If I can find one, it will be an airline run by women, with a name whose initials involve letters towards the back of the alphabet.

December 15th
Enlightened Capitalism? Sure, If It Makes Money

• •

• • • *Ampthill, England:* I pack much into a short visit to my home country. In three days I manage to do all my scenes for my new film (*The Full Monty: The Sequel*) and attend a celebrity party launching Elton John's new record tribute to the baby-shaking young lady who is some distance from being the toast of Boston. It's called *Goodbye English Nanny.* I also close my country house down for the winter. It will not be open to the public again until early April next year, unless, of course, another member of the royal family dies, in which case I will open the east wing, so that crowds can sign the condolence register for a small, dignified, fee.

An eerie feeling comes over me during the visit: I find myself liking our new (socialist) premier Tony Blair.[2] It is now almost 15 years since Margaret Thatcher started the practice of weekly phone calls with me to review strategy and, frankly, I think both the country and I suffered when I refused to continue them with John Major (such a nice man, but allergic to victory of any kind). Blair, however, wisely asked me to begin again, and I decided to give it a whirl. I confess I was delighted when he immediately took my advice on Scottish devolution, empowering the Bank of England, and the funeral arrangements for Princess Diana. Such a *nice* touch to have them walking behind.

Much has been made of Blair's similarity with Clinton, but I believe he has little in common with the latter and his Reign of Terror. They are both, I suppose, media-savvy, and it is true that their wives exemplify New Womanhood. I guess a case could also be made that all their children wear strange wigs—but there the similarity ends. It is essential to Bill's survival that he attempts no big programs, whereas Tony plans nothing else. Blair also seems to understand basic cause-and-effect factors in macro-economics, while Clinton basks in the glory of America's strongest ever economy without exhibiting a clue as to why it should be so. Luckily, it seems to be in safe hands: those of Robert Rubin and Alan Greenspan.

What the Democrat and Labour parties do have in common is that they were both swept to power via a public backlash against the Darwinist excesses of Reaganism/Thatcherism, but the early signs of both regimes show no indications of reversing the economic fundamentals of their inheritance. In reality, their respective portfolios include budget tightening and welfare reform proposals normally associated with their dogmatic opponents. Quite cleverly they have decided not to change *what* goes on, but signaled differences in *how* we go about it. It is a kinder, gentler—more inclu-

---

2. In 1997 Tony Blair and his 'new' Labour Party swept to power after 18 years of Conservative government.

sive—approach, with more attention paid to the needs of the least able and infirm.

Will business take a lead from Bill and Tony? Still prepared to take those ruthless competitive decisions, will we see captains of industry now become a tad more gentle in their execution? Will corporations accept they reflect stakeholdings by employees and communities as well as investors? God forbid the accountants would ever condone it, but will we begin to treat people as assets not expenses?

God forbid the accountants would ever condone it, but will we begin to treat people as assets not expenses?

If we do, it will (sadly) not come from political inspiration. It never has; it never will. If it comes, it will be driven by the force that has driven every inch of forward movement in capitalism: *vested self interest*. If it helps earnings per share, do it.

There continue to be a limited number of business leaders who give such signals of inspiration from within industry: that you can actually care for, and reward, your people differently *and take the results to the bank*. If you read the phenomenal success story of Howard Schultz and Starbucks (*Put Your Heart Into It,* Hyperion Books, 1998) you will read of a guy who insisted on diluting his company's share base to give *all* employees a stake in the company, and who added to his discretionary cost base by providing them with benefits. Both actions were against the collective wisdom of the retail industry, and both inhibited the company's short-term results. The rest, as they say, is history.

Before I leave England, I find time to start a frivolous rumor about one of the Spice Girls (Baby Spice, I think) and their founding manager, a Mr. Simon Fuller. By the time I de-plane in Florida, I find the group damaged beyond recovery and their collective careers spiraling downwards. Fairly shortly afterwards, one of them leaves (Licorice Spice, I think). Several more get pregnant. The end is near. Score one for the boomers.

December 29th
What's Ahead In 1998

• •

• • • *January*: PepsiCo announce the $700 million launch of 'New Pepsi.' Rather strangely, they withdraw it after three hours on the market, and announce they are replacing it with 'Classic Pepsi.' A company spokesperson explains, 'If it worked for them ….'

February: Microsoft and Starbucks announce a joint venture; the new Windows 98 will produce a double latte with skimmed milk from a special port on the side of your PC. Janet Reno slaps another $1 million-a-day fine on Microsoft for 'anti-competitive practices.' Bill Gates doesn't notice this one either.

March: Moodys lowers the City of Miami's bond rating to 'somewhere between PP and RR'; apparently on a level with Bosnia and Luton Town Football Club.

April: A council of Swiss bankers sadly have to postpone a meeting which was to have begun the process of paying compensation to holocaust victims from deposits of Nazi gold. Apparently, the 8-year-old son of one of the members had a big soccer match. The meeting is re-scheduled for July 2003. Meanwhile another 130 holocaust survivors die of old age. That leaves 69 to go.

May: In a further consolidation of the worlds telecommunication industry, Cuba buys BellSouth. At a press conference in Havana, spokesperson Fidel Castro explained that there would be 'a lot of phone business in this area after I'm gone.' Asked (politely) when that would be, he replied mysteriously that he'd seen *Alien Resurrection*.

June: Ruling on a case that is now recognized as being about much more than infanticide, the New England Appeal Court rule that the 'Nanny' verdict shall be determined by a soccer match to be played between England and the US. England win 4–3, and declare a national holiday.

July: Moodys downgrades Miami's bond rating to ZZ; level with the MIR space station.

August: 'Chainsaw' Albert Dunlap acquires a chain of hot dog stalls, and immediately fires *all* serving staff. Sales slump to zero, but the stock soars on the first day of trading. 'We're now the industry's lowest cost producer,' roars Al. 'And we will continue to focus on stockholder value and nothing else.' The stock doubles again on day 2.

September: The Equal Employment Opportunity Commission bring another lawsuit against Miami's landmark 'Joe's' Stone Crab restaurant. The percentage of stone crab legs *from female crabs* does not reflect the overall gender demographics of Dade County. After a trial costing the taxpayer several million dollars, EEOC inspectors join Joe's buying team to make sure enough female crab legs are included in future. Nobody knows quite how to do this.

October: Using only paper stock, Wayne Huizenga acquires General Motors for AutoNation. Part of the deal involves the re-naming of Detroit after a suitable sponsor has been found.

November: Sadly, the last—and biggest—of the Japanese finance houses collapses. The company hire Kenneth Branagh and disguise him as a Japanese CEO to deliver the close-down speech at the press conference. Sales of Kleenex soar. Elton John issues a commemorative record: *Goodbye Tokyo Rose*.

December: A small, independent, British film gains an unprecedented 23 Oscar nominations. It tells the story of the adult years of Diana, Princess of Wales, and is entitled *One Wedding and a Funeral*.

1998

There Is No Hope

• •

• • • *Black Mountains, Wales*: It is the dawning of the Age of Aquarius and (as an Aquarian) I decide on a period of solitude to ponder the implications for business. I decide to live rough for a winter week or so in these glorious hills, and eat only some stolen honey, a few edible roots, and a small mountain lion (previously thought to be extinct) that I kill with my bare hands. I drink only melted ice, and sing ancient Welsh hymns to myself very quietly.

My inner peace is troubled by the state of the world of business as we reach this defining moment. Commerce has been around in a form we can recognize for more than a thousand years, but it stands at the doorway of this new age in a very sad state indeed; ripped by counter-pulling forces, unsmiling and appallingly directed. And that's just General Motors.

Strangely, the collective wisdom of the great minds of business believes that the biggest problem on the horizon is a technical one: that at the stroke of midnight on December 31st 1999 the world's computers will implode. As I understand it, the inability of some big CPUs to deal with a four-digit year identifier that begins with '2' will mean my credit card bills may not find their way back to me, my Internal Revenue file may be erased, and Rome's traffic management system may fail. As the latter never existed, and the first two sound cool to me, I think I need a further briefing on what the actual problem is.

I am still on my first day of my week of lonely reflection when I discard this as the biggest problem facing business. There are many others with profoundly darker implications. Interestingly, none of them are technical, but reflect on how the *spirit* of this whole thing has gone wrong over the last millennium. Business is now clearly one of the planet's biggest nightmares (along with ten-pin bowling and the plonker who invented *Riverdance*) and is riddled with such seminal paradoxes as:

- Consumers crave products and services of real distinction and added value. What has evolved is planet full of ho-hum ones. Have you flown in a commercial airline lately?

- The new dynamics of corporate change mean we need faster decision making. What has happened is that access to (almost) infinite data banks and analysis has enabled us to procrastinate with real sophistication.

- Of the 100 largest economies in the world, almost exactly half are corporations. However, of the 50 or so countries on the list only a couple are not democracies; *none* of the corporations are. (Just imagine the impact if one of the countries expelled—i.e. downsized—a few thousand citizens.)

- Whether you employ thousands of people or just three, you need them to be savvy and motivated. What have we got? The most alienated workforces ever.

Whether you employ thousands of people or just three, you need them to be savvy and motivated

Sadly, we have nowhere to look for help. Our business school professors, mired in their tenureships, ramble on about the hierarchical needs of the individual, while the individual worries about car payments. Our elitist, fat-cat, mass-firing, business-leader role models are clearly no help either. The ordinary employee is also in a lost world: if you saw two stone cutters doing *exactly* the same work, one would define it as cutting stone into blocks while the other would probably spout on about being a member of a diverse group adding value to reusable resources while pursuing the success criteria of building a cathedral.

The astonishing and scary truth is that there is no one to look to but me. I emerge from my week's search for my inner self refreshed and ready to face the challenge of leading the world of business to a better tomorrow (charging only reasonable fees for services rendered). Suddenly my calm is shattered as I am hit by a *staggering* blow. Once again, I have been beaten in the race to be *Time* magazine's Man of the Year, this time by Intel's Andy Grove (he of the high profile prostate and paranoia). How can this be? How can it keep happening? Who *cares* how many million transistors Andy Groves can jam on his bloody bing-bong-bing-bong Pentium whatsit. Don't you folk who vote for this stuff realize I can't save modern business if I don't feel *appreciated*? Is it *too* much to ask?

I'm sulking now and I'm going back up the mountain just as soon as I can find my Swiss army knife. I'll let you know how I get on.

January 26th
Branding Over Troubled Waters

• •

• • • They telephone me in the early hours to tell me of Paul Simon's Broadway disaster with *Capeman*, but I am not sad for him. Far from it.

Not many people know he wrote *Bridge Over Troubled Water* in 1970 to celebrate one of my earliest (and some say one of my best) mid-life crises, and many is the hour we have since spent talking to each other on our cellular phones, shaping his destiny. He was forever grateful for the advice I gave him: i.e. that he should leave Arthur and go solo. That advice was given, by the way, the same week I advised Dylan to go 'electric.'

Paul Simon will be back, with this misstep behind him. It is a small price to pay for the constant reinvention and restlessness that are the characteristics of a long-term winner. This is not the kind of artist who has sung *American Pie* every night for 30 years.

Apart from his musical talent, he is also a magnificent example of modern branding, and should be the subject of a case study in every business school. Keeping his same brand name and core attributes, his constant (risky) self reinvention has kept him relevant, distinct, and successful in one of the most competitive markets on earth.

Branding is getting more complex as a science, and is clearly beyond the understanding of our Generation-X, who are now largely educated by ticking multiple-choice boxes. If you are an average American (and here I exclude Charlie Sheen), yesterday you were exposed to between 2000 and 3000 brand messages, on radio, TV, billboards, Internet, print, clothing labels, food packaging, store signs, and so on. I bet you can't remember *one*. (See?) And yet billions of dollars were spent in getting these messages to you. Was it *all* wasted? You can't tick a box to get the right answer here; it's too subtle.

Yesterday you were exposed to 2000–3000 brand messages, on radio, TV, billboards, Internet, print, clothing labels, food packaging, store signs, and so on

Branding has changed profoundly in the 1990s. Four decades of post-war prosperity left us sloppy in our buying habits, and easily swayed by 'mass-marketing' techniques. For many of us, job security and positive equity in our homes gave us a false sense of security and a poor sense of (real) value, but the deep recession at the turn of the 1980s, plus the massive technology-driven clear-out of white-collar jobs, changed all that. We began to buy *wisely*, reflecting our own personal values, and not those somebody intimated we should have. New branding signaled its arrival on an historic day in 1992, when Marlboro (a classic post-war brand model) dropped prices in response to losing share to unbranded cigarettes. I don't know what the word is for the opposite of an orgasm, but (whatever it is) Wall Street certainly had one that day.

Branding didn't die, but it had to change. Price did *not* become the sole determining factor, but brand owners had to recognize that the cocktail mix of product/price/service that they offered their consumers had to offer substantive *value*, and that they needed to custom-tailor the mix more towards the individual than ever before. That's why service, and the *relationship* established with the customer, became such a *key* differentiator in the market place; it's the easiest one to individualize. In a decade, we have moved from mass marketing to (almost) mass customization.

Something else changed, too. Branding stopped being about simply products, and became more about 'attributes.' Virgin (who threaten to become Britain's first *new* world-wide brand for 50 years) led the thinking here, believing they have core business attributes of 'fun,' 'innovation,' and 'great value,' which they can successfully deliver across a wide portfolio of products (air travel, music, soft drinks, financial services, and so on). The logic here is that people who are comfortable with these attributes are more likely to try or buy their products. If this is right, it helps explain Burger King's current US success at the expense of McDonald's, Sears resurrection, the slow demise of Laura Ashley, Nordstrom's dominance, and the mess that is still Kmart.

Branding stopped being about simply products, and became more about 'attributes'

The good thing about branding is that some mystery still exists, so there is still room for the creative genius to score a great victory. For example: I have particular needs for a wristwatch, which is something I rely on *hugely*. I don't like expensive ones (I live in Miami, you get mugged); I like analogue faces, luminous hands (for when I wake up in the middle of the night in strange hotels), figures (including a date) I can read without my eyeglasses, and a style that I can wear with jeans or a suit. I replaced mine recently with a brand that captured them all: the Swiss army watch. Then I just laughed. Such an important thing in my life, so why would I buy something branded after one of the most *irrelevant things in history?*

Then I went to put on my Jerry Garcia necktie, branded after a *four-fingered guitarist* who never wore a necktie in his life. I have three of them. Does anybody know why I do these things?

February 9th
My ECU's Bigger Than Yours

• •

• • • The uninformed US business person looks on at the goings-on in Asia (economic meltdown) and Europe (the European Union) with a range of emotions, the main one being complete indifference. After four bottles of champagne and a small omelet, I have decided to explain it all to you.

The first one, Asia, is easy. What's gone wrong is that Japan hasn't had a war (which boosts any economy) for 50 years, so my solution is for them to have one. Only this time we don't want any of that Pearl Harbor rubbish, leastwise not near us, so they should declare war on Iraq. That will put a stop to this monthly crisis where Saddam (the Arabian Wayne Newton) plays silly buggers and then backs down just before we give the order to the war planes to go and bomb him into a sticky black paste. If Japan took the job on, within a few weeks of being on a full war footing, the Nippon economy would be buoyant, loans would be repaid, they'd be buying our bonds again, and their tourists would be everywhere. Then all Asia will thrive again. Unfortunately, they would also be competing again, only now with devalued currencies. Saddam? He'll be weighing in at about 75 pounds, and helping to building a railroad somewhere in a jungle.

Europe presents a different picture. Almost every aspect of the post-independence relationship between the Old and New World has been synergistic, highlighted by our allied struggle against tyranny in the two world wars (where France claimed home court advantage throughout the play-offs in both series). Leaving German war-mongering aside, there have been few examples of it going wrong; an exception proving the rule being after World War I, when Woodrow Wilson and his cronies managed to guarantee a second great war (by insulting Japan and financially crushing Germany). While they were at it, they probably sewed the seeds for the next century's Holy War by 'inventing' Yugoslavia.

The relationship, however, has generally benefited both continents, particularly in business, where each offers the other both a source *and* market for products/services, investment, brains, and skills. The varieties in all of these, thrown up by the sheer size and range of both continents, have nourished it further. Now we have a European Union, and I fear for the relationship and the synergy.

The EU is the first attempt since Charlemagne (c. AD750) to unite Europe for 'positive' reasons. It has failed, and will continue to do so. The people don't want it, and it provides nothing that could not be provided to all nations by the UN—a global, economic, military and human rights superstructure. What have developed are more layers of confusion, expense, and regulation, providing barriers to business development and trade for members and external partners alike. Within the borders of the EU, *nothing* is achieved that could not be achieved by sensible world free-market development (e.g. in telecommunications and financial services, etc.), and

The EU is the first attempt since Charlemagne to unite Europe for 'positive' reasons—it has failed, and will continue to do so

a sensible international approach to govern the movement of capital and labor. Monetary union (within the EU) will prove a joke, with 'my ECU is worth more than yours' taking over from the current exchange mechanisms.

Europe does contain some of the most gloomy sights on earth (the war graves in northern France, the entrance to EuroDisney, and Michael *Riverdance* Flatley are each capable of depressing me for weeks), but it remains a glorious mosaic, and a *celebration* of true variety. I love those loopy French banknotes, and the way the Spanish eat dinner when the rest of the world is going to bed. Germany brews the finest beer in the world, and it should be *just fine* with all of us if they want to keep doing so. The Dutch have been business visionaries since the early 1600s, when they invented a derivative market for tulips (wow). And how can you not admire the Italians? Italy declared war in 1940 with its leader (Mussolini) convinced he had 5 million men in his army? In fact he had less than a million, and wouldn't you have just *loved* to be the guy who broke the news to him? But for all the fun you can have with the Italian war record, the world loves their food, and they bow to no one on the soccer field. Scratch *any* Irishman and you find a poet. Only in my home country could you find something as dotty and delightful as a 'Sir' Elton John. Belgium is also unique: nobody famous has *ever* been born there.

From a business vantage point, all of them are wonderful markets for the US, and provide sources for a rich variety of inputs and influences to commercial life over here. Help us stop the *federalists* and *celebrate* the differences; it is in *all* our interests.

On behalf of all Europe, I'll offer the American people a deal, as a precursor to the kind of opportunities that lie ahead. If you'll forgive us for Van Morrison, we'll forgive you for putting ketchup on your *nouvelle cuisine*.

February 23rd
Cooking Profits?

• •

• • • 'Tis the season for fourth quarter corporate earnings, and the business channels on TV are full of them, which is odd because they ought to be on the Food Channel.

Since the first stockbrokers appeared in England in 1637 (followed 100 years later by guys doing the same thing around the Buttonwood tree on Wall Street), business leaders have been inflating profits to impress the market makers. In short, they cook the books in ways that range from a gentle simmer to a deep roast. I've done it myself, as has *anybody* responsible for a big chunk of public company earnings. Although I'd claim to be a gentle 'simmerer,' it was a crowded kitchen.

There are four ways it happens, and I'll start with the most dangerous. All business leaders manage the bottom line as a priority, with their actual business (retail, production, wholesaling, whatever) a poor second. That's fine and mostly harmless, but it becomes dangerous when internal goals are not delegated, and management is left alone to execute them. The 1990s produced a classic example of how nasty this can become. A *Business Week* investigation into Bausch and Lomb (the parent company for Ray Ban sunglasses) revealed that their audited accounts for 1993 and 94 hid a mess. Targets were handed down without debate by paranoid and demented leaders, with failure to deliver resulting in dismissal. The result? Non-existent sales were booked at the year end, and distributors were forced to take up to two years' stock. Receivables were then factored and product dumped on the black market; nasty, nasty stuff, culminating in the market value of the company halving and a lot of senior corporate funerals before it was cleared up. The rule: if you don't delegate *'what'* has to be done, don't delegate *'how'* it gets done either.

Unhealthy earnings can also result from myopic pricing, which supports short-term revenues but is unsustainable. The traditional 'cost-plus' approach to pricing (the reason why the west has no consumer electronics industry) is one way this can go wrong, but so can a dumb insistence that you can 'premium price' when you can't. When Burger King's sales were soft at the end of the 1980s, many operators responded to the drop in revenues by (duh!) *raising* menu prices. Everybody was then astonished when revenues dropped even further. The rule: price led costing is the *only* sustainable price model.

Wall Street, of course, loves the third category of unhealthy earnings: the big 'downsize,' or corporate 'crash diet,' where thousands of buffalo (oops! sorry—*employees*) are slaughtered overnight. There is increasing evidence, however, that this does not always produce healthy earnings increases. Indeed, studies in the 1990s are showing that often the projected profit and productivity increases do not come through at all, but, even if they do, companies may pay a heavy future price. *The Economist* cites the cases of Delta Airlines and Nynex, both of whom downsized dramatically in the early 1990s. Delta lost its service edge, and Nynex ended up paying customers a rebate for poor service. Increasing evidence shows that companies also lose vast intangible assets; the contacts, know-how, experience (etc.) of those departed. The loss can prove costly.

We all know the last one: the manipulation of a company's discretionary costs such as travel, marketing, recruitment, office supplies, etc.—all those things that can be turned off quickly. It's a rare company that doesn't put the brake on these expenses in the last weeks of the financial year, with some doing it as early as month 2. The problem is, it becomes addictive. If you do it one year, you find you need to repeat it. My rule: if your discretionary costs in the first two months of the year are more than twice the level they are in the last two, it's a symptom hiding a disease. Stop and fix the disease.

My rule: if your discretionary costs in the first two months of the year are more than twice the level they are in the last two, it's a symptom hiding a disease

If you have responsibility for big profits in a public company, and do none of these, go study yourself in the mirror. You are unique. I also suspect you spray the lavatory with air freshener *before* you visit.

You should also write to Pope John The Bestseller, c/o The Vatican. There is a strong chance you could be canonized for this behavior—about seven centuries from now, so don't get *too* excited.

March 9th
Out Of Africa?

• •

• • • *Tamboerskloof, Cape Town, Southern Africa:* In 1958, when I was 12, I fell in love with an older man. He was Brazilian and 17 years old, his name was Pele, and during the World Cup finals of that year, he gloriously reinvented soccer.

Quite simply, he was black—as this was before more complex racial definitions (such as African-Cockney) had become *de rigeur*. I would have been delighted to have had him as my school buddy or neighbor. As my childhood was in England, it was not until my late teens that I realized that other parts of the planet were imploding with legalized racism.

Racism did exist in England (and still does—I'm not that daft), but it was illegal and away from the front pages. That's not surprising considering the island's history, with Iberians, Celts, Norsemen, Angles, Saxons, and Romans all coming and going in our distant past, and Irish, Hebrews, and the citizens of our latter-day 'Empire' drifting on and off stage in more recent times. Our first civil rights legislation, the Magna Carta, hit the statute books in 1215.

The late 1950s brought TV into our homes, and I personally used several thousand tons of hair gel, and damaged a knee cartilage, in my (fruitless) pursuit of looking and moving like Elvis. I also became acutely, and uncomfortably, aware of some other flickering black and white TV images crossing the Atlantic. I saw bewildering scenes of riots at legally segregated lunch counters, buses, and schools, as US civil rights legislation crawled agonizingly towards the president's signature in the 1960s. Although I didn't realize it at the time, I also witnessed business miss a huge chance to develop another role in society, other than just wealth creation.

I also witnessed business miss a huge chance to develop another role in society, other than just wealth creation

South Africa, today, has recreated the American south of the 1960s. Legislation has been enacted and discrimination is illegal. Some are determined to make it work, some to make it fail, and others are just watching and waiting. It is hard to be optimistic, for the circumstances are more difficult than existed in the US of the 1960s: the oppression lasted longer; there are 'intra' as well as 'inter' racial issues; and extreme change happened very quickly. The US also had nothing like the 'townships': mile upon mile of horrendous shanty towns, housing literally millions of (largely) black and 'colored' no-hopers, positioned just outside the prosperous cities. This is the nearest thing I have seen, in my sheltered life, to living on a social San Andreas Fault.

Progress, in these circumstances, will always be too fast for one side, too slow for the other. In business, the 'mechanisms' to force corrective action and bring about employment equality (mandates, quotas, affirmative action programs, etc.) are recognized as imperfect but sometimes necessary. Mandela's South African government, however, have shown that they have learned *something* from the US experience, where the legal enthusiasm for not only telling you *what* you must do, but also *how* you must do it has often caused more problems than it solved. Under South Africa's Employment Equity Bill, employers are required to submit their *own* proposals on how they will achieve equity, reflecting their own particular circumstances, problems, and opportunities. Common sense from a government—whatever next?

South African business, however, faces more structural, long-term, problems than the US or UK ever did, but disguised as a profound problem is an enormous opportunity. The South African workforce is largely illiterate, with the exception being its (largely) white management cadre. They themselves need to change their whole skill base, moving from a world cocooned by international sanctions to one of open global competition. *What a huge opportunity* for business to undertake a unique and unprecedented role in society, working with government on a 5–20 year program to educate a generation. In the same way that Germany was able to rebuild its manufacturing base from scratch after 1945 (and, in so doing, achieve competitive advantage by investing in modern plant and machinery), so could South Africa with a parallel investment in modern training and education. It would be an historic first for business to do this, and it would need a sustained and significant investment in money and effort to achieve it, but the returns could be spectacular. The sad truth is that the rest of western education and training is poor and in decline, and is there to be beaten.

I gotta stop. This is all too serious for me, but it's tough to be lighthearted about this subject. You will be pleased to know, however, that my next travels take me back to Europe, where I will be covering the much lighter subject of the World Worm-Charming Championships in Nantwich, England. This is for real. Even I couldn't invent that.

March 23rd
The Business Year So Far (I Must Not SMEF!)

• • • It's proving to be a normal, tranquil, secure, orderly year in the world of business; same as normal, really. Here's my highlight reel so far:

- Wall Street confirms my view that it should move about 40 blocks north to Broadway; it provides much better entertainment. The market makers boast they know many companies *better* than the executives who work in them, and that their knowledge of what's going on, even in some tiny companies, is unparalleled. Meanwhile, Intel, one of the world's largest earners, has been giving off recent signals that earnings are likely to come in below expectation, and giving them off with the sort of subtlety that you see towed behind a small airplane over a football stadium. *Thursday 5th March*: Intel announce reduced earnings! Wall Street has a cow; they are bewildered, astonished, and mortified, all at once. They dump the stock (down $11.00) and drag the world's stock markets down. Then they buy it back the next day.

- The 2000 computer snafu will *not* be solved by the year 2000; more likely 2003–5. Add to that the one nobody has really thought about yet—the move to a (new) single European currency, which has *huge* worldwide computing implications— and you can plan a fun time in IT early next century.

- As many of you know, as a WASPM, I run a small dating agency in Miami. I recently fixed up SmithKline Beecham and Glaxo Wellcome in what would have been one of the biggest marriages in history. I normally retreat when the parties get engaged, and did so this time. What normally happens then is that the two parties have a glass or two of Chardonnay, and (with total integrity) decide they should sleep together before the actual marriage, just to be sure they are *truly* compatible. I *think* that's what happened here, because the next thing we saw is the two of them running like hell from each other. I wonder which one snored?

- *Book of the year so far:* Peter Bernstein's *Against the Gods* (John Wiley & Sons). Not really business, but the remarkable story of how mankind has managed risk throughout history, and the techniques developed to do so. It reminded me of when I first appeared in senior management, when risk was there to be enjoyed, and the challenge was to manage and reduce it. Now, we are driven by the *fear* of risk, as the litigious consequences of things going wrong are horrendous. As a result, we live in a world where lawyers, *de facto*, now take

We are driven by the fear of risk, as the litigious consequences of things going wrong are horrendous

about 80% of the business decisions that should be taken by managers.

- *Fall from grace of the year (so far): How* did Motorola stumble so badly from its market domination of 2–3 years ago? Part of the answer might be that a company called Lucent Technologies is winning share from it, and I spoke to Lucent's sales force only a few months ago. So, ignore me at your peril! I do Bar-mitzvahs and weddings (including an impersonation of Kenneth Starr impersonating Elvis).

- *'WOW!' experience of the year:* searching for a book out of print, Amazon's website service is unbelievable. 'We'll find it for you, second hand if necessary—and then we'll email you, telling you of its condition and price. Give us two months.' We've not fully digested it yet, but cyberspace will change *all* our lives profoundly over the next decade. It will take its place in history alongside the plough, the steam engine, the transistor, and the Wonderbra.

  We've not fully digested it yet, but cyberspace will change all our lives profoundly over the next decade

- I've had a home in Miami for 10 years now, but never held myself up as anything more than a foreigner (or 'resident alien' as the my immigration line is defined at Miami's airport), or a Johnny-come-lately. However, even I (*moi!*) got annoyed when Miami's latest political fiasco was the highlight of a TV show I watched from a hotel bed in California. What's my business point? Business takes a lot of hits, many deserved. But in *any* public company I have known, or known of, on either side of the Atlantic, these mouth-breathers and felons would not last two weeks.

- *Business concept of the year:* a SMEF (Spontaneous Massive Existence Failure) in Terry Jones's (ex-*Monty Python*) hilarious sci-fi story of the 'Starship Titanic' Avoidance of a SMEF should be a cornerstone of all these stupid mission statements companies keep coming up with. Fingers crossed that PanAm avoids SMEFing (and thus joining some other great names of the past who have SMEFed).

April 6th
Mission Impossible?

• •

• • • Bad news: my phone rang at 3:00 a.m. It was Saddam Hussein (forgetting the time difference between Miami and Baghdad again) and he was not happy—telling me angrily that our public relations plan wasn't working. The plan referred to was something I put together for him a while back, when he first called about his frustration at not being respected by the people of the world (including most Iraqis), and I suggested he go online (*shussein@ donkeywalloper.com*) to expose his humility and integrity via a chat room. The problem with Saddam is simple: charisma. Or, rather, lack of it. If you stand too near him, you can hear the ocean. Ah, well.

As if that wasn't enough, Queen Elizabeth faxed me three hours later with the same problem. Since the funeral of you-know-who, and the royal family's carefully planned positioning (which got *everything* wrong), she, too, has been trying to get closer to 'her' people. She was wondering whether her idea of not insisting on everybody bowing or curtseying when first in her presence was (perhaps) a little *too* much, *too* fast? I tell her that I think it is. This is a lady who has a knack of making strangers immediately, but the people must have structure.

Such folk seek me out because I was one of post-industrial society's great popular leaders. In particular, the US Burger King franchisees worshipped me—and whenever I would visit their locations they would arrange a public holiday, garland the streets with flowers, hire marching bands, and often sacrifice a small warm blooded animal (or even a maiden if it was in the *deep* south). Now, I sell my secrets via a worldwide consultancy.

Just what is it that makes some business leaders widely respected, and others scorned? Why is it that, whereas *both* Jack Welch and Albert Dunlap are successful, and thus revered by Wall Street, only one of them is respected by a universal audience? (Our attorneys asked me to leave this to you to work out for yourselves.) My advice is that business success is only a starting point, and there are then four more ingredients business leaders have to achieve the broad acclaim craved by many, but achieved by few.

First, they are *multi-dimensional:* They build revenues as well as cut costs; they are at ease in the shipping department at midnight as well as the boardroom; they are balanced with lives outside the company; they respect *all* the stakeholders in a business; they support as well as control; and they plan for the long term and deliver in the short. No one-trick ponies make this list.

They are also *accessible:* Well past the age when most leaders have retired, Sam Walton kept up a punishing schedule of store visits across America *every week*. However busy these guys are, they make time to see (and be seen in) the business. Today, they often have open access on email and voice-mail, and respond *personally*. MBWA (Management By Wandering About) is an essential element in this, and, in times when leadership pressures are intense and calendars structured for months in advance, this is tough.

They are more than just good communicators, they are sound-sensitive— they have spectacular listening skills They are more than just good communicators, they are *sound-sensitive*: They have spectacular listening skills. They encourage challenge and contribution from anyone, everywhere, and find ways to receive those signals. God gave them two eyes, two ears and one mouth: four organs for receiving and one for transmitting information, and that's the ratio they use. Furthermore, if they are aware of a pocket of discontent in the business, that's their first port of call, not the last.

These folk are *non-elitist*. That is *not* the same as egalitarian, and— although much is written today about leaders who operate out of a cubicle, fly coach class, and insist on the same working conditions for everybody in the business—there is a subtle difference. Leadership jobs *are* different, just as *all* jobs in the company are. To 'force' equality is dumb—Sam Walton could not have done his job his way without a private plane—but there is a *huge* difference between making sure every job in the company has the appropriate facilities, support, and infrastructure to be effective, and the crass 'limo-to-the-bathroom' elitism that is endemic with many business leaders. Our guys pitch it right, and as a result their companies are about 'we' and not 'us and them.'

Looking back, on my good days I showed bits of all four, but there were too many days when too many were missing. So now I am an expert consultant in the subject. Whoops! There goes the phone again. Let's look at Caller ID ... wow ... Kenneth Starr. Here's a guy who gives every indication that he has been working with glue too much. *This* one will be a challenge.

I Say To-mah-to, You Say To-may-to

• • • Back in England for a short visit to oversee some exciting developments to our country house. We have completely redecorated a bedroom in the east wing, and re-named the room the Diana, Princess of Wales Suite. Everybody in England has one now, and it can only be a matter of time before this latest Cool Britannia trend sweeps the US.

As part of the project we bought a couple of grand's worth of antique furniture, and had an astonishing experience. Having agreed on a price, and *not* to pay by credit card (the dealer's wish), we paid by check.

Have you ever tried to pay by check in Miami? You need to be accompanied by your banker, accountant, and old high school Principal. You need to give a blood sample and your last six tax returns, and have the driving licenses of at least twelve relatives (besides yours). You will have to leave your first born as collateral until the check clears, and all this will get you clearance up to $30.

For the furniture in England, I signed the check and gave it to the dealer. He then asked us where they would deliver it *that afternoon*. When I queried whether they would hold the delivery until the check cleared, we were cheerfully informed that they trusted us. Wow.

It highlighted again some of the differences in doing business on either side of the Atlantic, and I write about it with some trepidation. I gave an interview to a business magazine recently, and, via a collection of misquotes and a load of editorial omissions, they neatly turned my views into a catalog of who was better and who was worse. For six months I had to hide in a neutral country. People get pissed off with this stuff.

There *are* differences, but they are not about being better or worse. Frankly, and rather sadly, they are no longer sizable, and the gap is narrowing. A normal bell-curve of business behavior finds the bulk of both countries' business people in the bulk of the bell, but the *extremes* of attitude and activity are at one end of the curve in the US and at the other in the UK.

The US is now the least-trusting business climate on earth Take this trust thing as an example. The US is now the least-trusting business climate on earth. It is a great sadness of modern commercial life (and one of the many reasons why I abandoned Big Business) that the handshake has ceased to mean anything. Teams of lawyers are needed to consummate the simplest transactions.

At the heart of this is a deep difference in philosophy. In the UK (and Europe) there is a continuing assumption that, once agreement has been reached, both parties will try to make it work as planned. In the US the assumption is that the other guy will try and screw you from the minute the ink is dry.

The international nature of business today means that most business cultures are the same on both sides of the pond; i.e. *highly untrusting*. But at the extremes, a refreshing (but vulnerable) naiveté can be found in the UK, while a frustrating (and often counter-productive) bureaucracy can drive you mad in the US.

A similar pattern emerges in the Brave New World of political correctness. Again, much of the UK and the US is now under the grip of common practices that have *dramatically* changed attitudes and behavior over the past decade. But at the extremes, big differences remain. In the UK this extreme will make bad social decisions: in the US bad business decisions.

In the UK, for example, if you want to advertise for somebody to haul heavy bags by hand every day, the idea that you must allow pregnant women to apply on an equal footing with a healthy, unpregnant, young male is still considered fatuous. This may, of course, be a bad social decision. In the US however, the heavy handed interpretation of affirmative action, quotas, EEOC, ADA, etc., has resulted in some loopy business decisions.

American business people tend to love *activity*, whereas the Brits do not; at least, not for its own sake. An ex-colleague of mine, Gerry Robinson, now runs the enormous Granada conglomerate, and insists on a four-day week. Can you imagine *that* in the US corridors of power? In the US that is simply not the way: business life is a dawn-to-dusk, six days a week, 50 weeks a year, minute-by-structured-minute tapestry of to-do lists, written on yellow 'legal' pads, musical cell phones and beepers, emails, voice-mails, and therapy.

American business people tend to love activity, whereas the Brits do not

If there are any three-hour business lunches left on this miserable planet (apart from those happening in France where they remain *de rigeur*), they are probably happening with a few remaining die-hard business veterans in the square mile that is the City of London. They can be recognized by their noses, where the veins take on the appearance of a subway map. They are the folk who also miss the three-hour day. There are few left, very few. There are *none* in America.

I hope I have been diplomatic this time; for example, avoiding mentioning the Brits' generic hatred of anything with an Intel chip inside. I am, as they say, simply trying to celebrate one small aspect of the planet's diversity.

If you believe that of me, you will believe anything. So, I will leave you now, before I get into trouble. Besides, I am having difficulty in choosing the artist to lead the concert to open our new bedroom. I have Eric on line 1, and Elton on line 2. Neither will take 'No' for an answer.

May 4th
They Did It Their Way

• •

• • • Some decades ago I decided to try my hand at writing a song lyric. I had this wonderful line buzzing around my head, which went: 'And now, the end is near, and so I face the final curtain, da-da, dee-da-dee-da, dee-da-dee-da, (something) I'm certain.' I remember writing it down on a napkin (in a restaurant in Canada, I think) then losing it. It's a pity; maybe somebody could have done something with it.

I'm reminded of it again this spring as there seem to be a number of important final curtains coming down. Seinfield is going, and I'm under *strict* instructions from our attorneys not to reveal any details of my small cameo role in the big finale.[3] In addition, two of indus-

---

3.   It was cut. Bastards.

try's Big Cheeses are retiring: Bob Crandall of American Airlines, and Tony O'Reilly of Heinz. On the surface, these two have much in common: their businesses were successful, they were high-profile leaders, they didn't hide from controversy or tough decisions, they made themselves very wealthy, and they retired of their own accord. It is my belief, however, that history will view them differently: in O'Reilly's case very favorably, in Crandall's case much less so.

It takes a lot of varied skills to build brands, and it also takes a lot of courage—you have to think long term in a world driven by next quarter's earnings

I feel I know both men. I met O'Reilly a few times during my tenure at Burger King, as Heinz sold us many million dollars' worth of ketchup each year. (Or, as I pointed out to him, they didn't. What they sold to us was several million dollars' worth of little plastic 'condoms,' each holding a tiny amount of ketchup. He was polite enough to smile.) Of course I'm biased; he is from the land of my own father (Ireland) and was a schoolboy hero of mine in the only activity that unites that troubled isle (rugby). His performance as a brand builder has been phenomenal, from his early days in the Irish dairy industry to the modern 50 plus brand portfolio in the mighty Heinz empire (to say nothing of his recent parallel roles in rescuing and rebuilding the Wedgwood (fine pottery) and Waterford (fine crystal) brands. It takes a lot of varied skills to build brands, and it also takes a lot of courage. You have to think long term in a world driven by next quarter's earnings. I wish I had done more of it.

My relationship with Crandall is different; I never met him. But my American Airlines card notes I have flown 2 *million* miles with them over the past 10 years, so I feel I know him well. And I don't like what he, and a handful of his peers, have done to that industry. The brand is summed up in a recent experience I had with them, when I had to call in at American Airlines' Miami office to change a ticket. When I entered there were *no* other customers; just three employees behind the counter staring intently at their computer screens. I got no acknowledgment, no eye contact. When I asked (politely) for assistance I was told (are you ready?) to *take a number*. In fairness, what happened next[4] was probably my fault—

---

4. You really don't want to know.

but you get my drift. This is a pre-Copernicus brand that believes it is still the center of the universe. You see it now in almost every aspect of their product, pricing, attitude, and service, and they have the gall to tell me *it's really what I want*. Guys, I don't want a cheap bad experience. I want a cheap *good* experience.

I rate Crandall in the same way as Henry Ford. He seems to me capable of producing huge joy when he leaves a room. Many people canonize Ford for enormous macro wealth creation, bringing motorized mobility to the masses, and paying enhanced wages. For me, he took one of the wondrous experiences of the century (the motor car), and took it down to a level where it failed to meet customer's real aspirations. What it met was Ford's *arrogant assumptions* of those aspirations. Eventually, Ford lost its way and somebody else recovered that experience for the motorist. I hope some visionary will come along and do the same for air travel.

Crandall scores 5 out of 10 for doing more with less. O'Reilly scores 9 out of 10 for doing more *of better* with less. That's the stuff that makes real legends.

I know many of you will want to email me and disagree, but I must tell you I will be away for a while. I have checked into a monastery for the whole of next week as I have just been advised that McCauly Culkin, the child star of *Home Alone*, is *getting married* at the ripe old age of seventeen. I have an overwhelming need to sit on a bunk bed and stare into space.

May 18th

HR Blues

• •

• • • Grim faced bearers bring me the bad news, and I take to my bed. Eleven European countries have triggered the go-ahead for a single currency, and I am overcome. I cancel all vacations for my team of personal valets, and command them to bring a stream of anti-depressants, lightly boiled eggs, and Viagra to my chambers.

Why would we (Europeans) do this? Why would we hand two *huge* bonuses to the competing American economy on a plate? An alternative international currency will savage the value of the dollar over the long term, and make it so much more competitive. It will also force us to share responsibility for propping up tosser-economies all over the globe, as and when they implode. Sheer madness.

And if *that* weren't enough, my day worsens. The people who handle this stuff for me advise me that I am booked to work a business seminar, later this month, on a cruise ship, out of an English port, *with 400 European HR executives* on board. I may be the first recorded death by empowerment. Here's the next boat for James Cameron to film.

I am fast despairing of the Human **I am fast despairing of** Resource function. The original idea for **the Human Resource** the role was solid—to recruit, retain, and develop the right people for the company's game **function** plan—but it has morphed into something much less nutritional and much more corrosive. Its now only a tad behind the legal profession in blocking the arteries of western enterprise. The first problem with HR is that it feels it has to invent words; even its own title is a stupid and unnecessary replacement of the old (and perfectly adequate) 'Personnel.' What's the goal here? To help distinguish a human resource (i.e. what we would normally call a person) from a *non*-human resource? A Martian perhaps? Or a lump of iron-ore?

Remember, HR are the people who came up with the idea that *outsourcing saves money*; an idea that should be filed under 'Total Bollocks.' The real problems started, however, when HR then began inventing words like 'empowerment', and acting as though it was entirely *new* and they were responsible for it. Such a crock. The idea is as old as the hills, if you use the perfectly good names we already had for it. The 'invincible' Spanish Armada was defeated by a heavily outnumbered—but *empowered*—English navy in 1588. Although the English ships were fewer in number, they were faster and better equipped, their captains were *trusted to take decisions against an overall strategy*. Their leaders (including Queen Elizabeth I) were involved and responsive. Substitute 'business units' for 'ships' in the above and you have a magnificent model of 'empowerment' for modern business; about 400 years before HR 'invented' it.

Empowerment is simply another word for trust, but if we were to go back to using *that* perfectly good word, we would soon get into trouble. Because to trust, you have to respect, and that's a thinly spread jam in modern business. Managers don't respect employees, franchisees don't respect franchisers, staffers don't respect operators, investor's don't respect executive decision-makers, the sales guys hate the advertising agency and many cultural factions disrespect others. And vice-versa for all of the above. Many stakeholders in the same organization are more alienated from others than at any other time in history, and HR has become a symbol of that distrust and disrespect. It has, in fact, become the agent that *institutionalizes* most of it.

Empowerment is simply another word for trust Take a contract of employment as an example. Page after page states quite clearly how and why western companies won't trust someone *who is contemplating joining them*. Grievance procedures, disciplinary procedures, delegated authority manuals—if you're ever unsure about exactly how not to trust anybody, *HR will give you a book on it*. If (God forbid) I were ever to work for a big corporation again, I would be *terrified* of smiling at anybody for fear of defiling their HR defined rights or alienating some HR cultural no-go area.

It's many years since now since the gloriously demented Townshend suggested doing away with HR (Robert Townshend, *Up The Organization*, 1970). His solid logic was that it should be a manager's job to manage the people-related issues of the business and the team. Reality tells us that is no longer possible; the compliance complexities alone of modern employment mean that experts are needed. But in a world where the capability and commitment of the people you have seem *so* important in determining a company's market distinction, it seems astonishing that the function has ended up largely accentuating the negative. It *should* be so different.

And I'm sharing a boat with 400 HR people. I will, of course, be safe. Any iceberg of any caliber seeing this lot coming over the horizon will get out of the way fast. The alternative is to risk being roped in to a Diversity Workshop or, worse still, be directed to dress casually on Fridays.

June 1st
Please Please Me, Woh Yeah

• •

• • • When I was in my late teens I had this fantastic formula for success with the opposite sex. Every Saturday, in my hometown of Manchester, England, I would play rugby in the morning, reluctantly, for the school second team. In the afternoon I would explode with happiness and play soccer for a local team. The combination would guarantee leg cramps at some stage during the evening. I would rush home from the game, eat very little, and then go to the pub and drink *huge* amounts of beer. Then a bunch of us would go to a club and listen to a local band, drink more beer, look cool, and wait for the last dance. When that arrived I would hop (leg cramps) towards the prettiest girl I could see and offer her the *once-in-a-lifetime* opportunity of a dance with me, followed by the privilege (for her) of me taking her home. This scientific approach to mating failed *every single time*. I didn't spot the flaw till years later.

On one such Saturday, in a dingy club called the Oasis, the MC announced a German band. He wasn't sure of the name. When they were setting up, we realized he was talking through his back passage. They weren't German because we knew the drummer—a guy called Richard 'Ringo' Starkey—who played with a local band. It transpired he had joined a new group called The Beatles, who had just returned from a gig in Hamburg. Two minutes later John Lennon hit the first chords of *Twist and Shout*, blew the top of my head off, and began altering civilization.

They've fascinated me ever since—and they have a lot to teach business. They had a *hugely* successful period and then it was all over and they faced the a post-Beatle world, just as many companies have a golden period and then have to figure out how to follow it. Ringo adopted one strategic option and did *absolutely nothing new*, and the Beatles brand name was so strong it kept him afloat (after a fashion) for nearly 30 years.

If you look around you can find a bunch of Ringo-brands today: names that have had glorious runs, but now seem to be in cruise control. McDonald's seems to have been asleep in the US during the 1990s, Boeing looks bewildered, Nike is discovering that there is no soft landing when you stop being a cult, and Motorola and Nordic Track look to be sliding after appearing impregnable a couple of years ago.

The Ringo analogy is apt. These brands aren't failures—people still like them and they are big enough to make a lot of people jealous— but they seem to have lost impetus, and I suspect they are now

Defense is an understandable mind-set when you're big and/or experiencing a successful run, but it can be dangerous

better at defending than attacking. This is a strange phenomenon that sometimes threatens the successful, and I first became aware of it when I joined Shell in England in the 1960s. It was a successful company, with a big market share, but with almost every strategy geared to defense.

Defense is an understandable mind-set when you're big and/or experiencing a successful run, but it can be dangerous. Five hundred years ago, England eventually lost the 100 Years War[5] with France, despite having the world's dominant weapon: the longbow. The problem with the longbow was that you could defend magnificently with it, but couldn't attack. Eventually you lose.

McCartney, however, showed business another option. If you have a golden period and a wonderful brand name, treat both of them as a *start*, not an end. Keep trying things; keep growing. Make mistakes. (Remember Coca-Cola's New Coke and purchase of Columbia? Big mistakes, but ones from which they learned and became a better company.) In 1997, McCartney had a classical music hit as well as a rock album, and still fills stadiums 30 years later in one of the most cluttered competitive markets there is. Now think about Gillette, Microsoft, and Intel. These are brands who have already had golden days, but never stopped. Always aggressive, always growing: I suspect the words 'coast' and 'defend' are banned words with these folk.

Of course there are 'Georges' as well; brands like Laura Ashley that you know are really very 'talented,' but are also really boring. I'll leave my hero John alone. Most big brands, however, are either Pauls or Ringos, and the combination of constant restlessness and the institutionalization of discomfort is the only winning formula.

Now, I know you've been waiting patiently for me to tell you about the flaw in my mating ritual (as many of my younger male readers will be taking notes). It turned out to be my *hair*. You see, I only used a *single* handful of Brylcreem, when the spirit of the age demanded at least two. If you young guys follow the rest of the formula, I'm sure you will be OK.

---

5.   Now *that* is a war.

Let It Be, Let It Be

• •

• • • *Ampthill, England:* I bring devastating news from the Old World. One of the Spice Girls has quit (Old Spice, I think), and England is in chaos. The government has resigned, parts of the north are in a state of civil war, the stock market has crashed, and our nice Mr. Blair is rumored to have tried to shoot himself. He missed, hence the smile.

Outside my baronial home an ugly mob has gathered, held back for the moment only by my well filled moat and the muskets of my remaining servants. I fear the end is near.

I open my laptop, and find solace in my Windows operating system. I finalize my estate planning and insurance, wind up my financial affairs, pen a few notes to my loved ones, and email this to the *Miami Herald*. I decide to dedicate my last moments to the enabling wonders that Bill Gates and Microsoft have given us.

I find I suddenly stand alone. Everybody has now crossed the road to side with the goons in the US Department of Justice: Microsoft is too big, too successful, too unfair on its competitors, and is now some sort of public menace. Even *The Economist*, the world's last bastion of sound liberal economic thinking, joins in the chorus.

Microsoft stand accused of using their free-market monopoly of operating systems to 'force' the use of their own web-browser (a sort of 1990s version of 'We've got the only supply of horses in town, so you must buy your saddle from us as well'). The loopy solution proposed is that Microsoft provide their competitor's browser on their own operating system. (Hey, Mr. McDonald, you're too successful. We want you to sell the Burger King products as well ....) The alternative is a long drawn out legal battle, which will cost the taxpayer zillions.

I am no personal fan of Mr. Gates. If he's one of two people talking, and one looks bored, he's the other one. Anybody with a personal wealth approaching $50 billion, who spends $3 on a haircut and loves writing computer code, lives in a place beyond my personal rainbow. But I respect him, and believe what Microsoft has achieved—

What Microsoft has achieved—not only for its investors, but for America—is one of the phenomena of the last millennium

not only for its investors, but for America—is one of the phenomena of the last millennium. The march of microchip and telecommunications technology, and, with it, the ability to distribute data processing and on-line access to tiny personal computers, have been astonishing. But it would have had much less impact without user-friendly operating systems. *That's* the breakthrough that has enfranchised a generation of ordinary people with new technology, including me; although I still don't know what to do with the right-side clicker on my mouse.

Of course the brave nineteenth-century anti-trust Sherman Acts, and their descendants, still have a role to play in business, but not *cart-blanche*. Account needs to be taken of the maturity of the industry, imminent developments, perceived motives of the so-called perpetrators, the substance of the potential damage to the public, and (yes, even from me, a lifetime free-trader) the *national interest*. To apply them to Gates and Microsoft in the same way as they were (rightly) applied to Rockefeller's Standard Oil is just dumb. My observation is that Microsoft is guilty—of being caught in a 'breakthrough-vortex.' Huge leaps of progress suddenly presented themselves in new areas of technology, and these guys got sucked in, and proved faster, better, *and more enthusiastic* than any competitor. The wealth of this nation improved as a result.

The Internet is just starting a journey that will affect every life someday

What is more important, however, is that the journey has just begun. The Internet is just starting a journey that will affect every life someday. Voice-activation is nearly with us. *Huge* corporate research and development programs are needed, involving dollar amounts beyond the imagination of *whole nations* a generation ago. Companies like Microsoft are capable of doing it, but they need the revenues to plough back and the confidence that their risks will be rewarded. In my view, it's another five years before we should worry, and, yes, they will get *very* rich. But that's the American way, and you bet that's what their whining competitors would like as well. Of course, if Microsoft doesn't do it somebody else will, *just* as they did for consumer electronics—remember?

But, wait! It's gone quiet outside, and the mob has dispersed. A new distraction has grabbed the nation and the Spice Girls are forgotten. On the Monday morning you read this, England will be winning their opening match in the soccer world cup, beginning a month's journey that will surely end with that most glorious of all sports trophies coming home to us.[6] And you can follow our progress on your web browser of choice.

---

6. History recorded, shortly after this was written, that England lost in the relatively early rounds. To Argentina of all countries. There are many of us who would have traded our military 'victory' in the Falklands War for a reverse of this soccer result. Trust me.

June 29th
Benefiting From The Iceberg

• •

• • • I have been fascinated by disaster from my early childhood. This was a result, I think, of my father's nickname for me, which was 'Ti' (short for Titanic).

It is true that the voyage through my youth saw me hitting several (metaphoric) icebergs, and I began to shape my own disaster theory: not so much that you *had* to experience a disaster to achieve greatness, but the more mundane thesis that, should you be unfortunate to experience one, you could actually emerge from it in better shape than before.

I experimented with this idea when I was about 25 years old, using soccer as a laboratory. It remains a mystery to this day why I was never selected to play for England, although some say that the following two facts had something to do with it: about 80% of my calorific intake came from beer; and my body fat percentage hovered around the 50 mark. I had, however, a very respectable right foot, and disaster struck when I broke it one day. Lying in the hospital bed, I determined there and then that I would be a *better* player than before. I planned to really work on my *left* leg during recovery, so that I would become a more balanced, all-round player. Sure enough, within six months I had two useless legs and was dropped.

So it didn't work for soccer, but my theory was evolving. History indicated it might only work if it was a *serious* disaster. Probably the greatest (pound for pound) of these ever to hit England was the Black Death in 1350, killing *nearly half* the population. Farms were untilled, whole villages abandoned; but this nightmare itself sewed the seeds for a stronger country. Labor was suddenly in such short supply that the process of emancipation gathered a momentum that enabled the country to lead the drive to modern democracy. The unserviced farms had to be turned over to sheep grazing, paving the way for the country's leadership in textiles (which was catalytic for the industrial revolution) a few hundred years later.

IBM experienced almost an equivalent corporate disaster around the end of the 1980s, wiping about $70 billion of its market value. That noble company had become a joke. (Bill Gates accused them of building the world's heaviest airplane. My own observation was that they had built the biggest thing for the wrong reason since the Pyramids.) Hugely bloated, in the wrong markets doing the wrong things, they floundered at the bottom for a while, then came out with a new leadership, new direction and new determination, and more than recovered the fumble. I suspect it took an absolute disaster to force the abandonment of the old, and the adoption of the new: *a mini-crisis simply would not have forced these issues.*

Clearly the first priority in any disaster is to survive; first by stabilizing, then by repair. The nearest I have come to an experience of this nature was when Hurricane Andrew wiped out Burger King's HQ in 1992 (along with the homes of most of its corporate employees). Like any disaster you wouldn't wish it on anyone, but if you are a victim and *can* stabilize and recover, you will suddenly find yourself in a *unique* position to become a better business. You are forced to crystallize your priorities (realizing that 'big' issues such as 'Dress Down Friday' are really a load of bollocks) You will find yourself more articulate, energized, productive, and capable than you ever thought possible, and that shouldn't be a surprise. Great work *does* come out of disaster; memorable plays are often tragedies, and wonderful music is frequently about love-gone-wrong. Billy Connolly, the gloriously demented Scottish comedian, makes the point that some of his country's finest music was written after the Battle of Culloden (which the Scots lost disastrously). When they won (Bannockburn), the music was crap.

When you've got nothing, you've got nothing to lose—you may as well go for that dream you've had, but that your attorneys stopped

Most important: in a real disaster, your views of risk change. When you've got nothing, you've got nothing to lose. You may as well go for that dream you've had, but that your attorneys stopped. Your natural conservatism can take a hike. You can go for it. And if you can survive, and you can get yourself in that frame of mind, it is no wonder you can make good, because you're on your own in western business for a short, glorious period.

Now I must take my disaster theory and apply it carefully to my great hero, Albert Dunlap (motto: 'Success in spite of management'), the great Turnaround Champ, lately fired by Sunbeam. At least I will when my pen stops shaking with my laughter. Damn these tears, I need a tissue.

July 13th

Lessons From Strange Places

• •

• • • In an effort to provide an antidote to the emotional inconti-
nence that has been evident in England since the death of you-
know-who, and to support the attempt to make the royal family
more user-friendly, I have been appointed mentor to Prince William.

So far, much of our time together has seen me drawing on my
wisdom to throw a fire blanket on the young man's exploding hormones, but he surprised me this week by asking some deep questions about business. Apparently, his father is keen that he 'serves
some time' in modern industry, all the better to 'be in touch with
the people' when he eventually takes up his proper job (i.e. King).
He fed me his father's initial advice: that one can *only* understand

business if one learns from business schools, business people, and business experience. From my kneeling position, I tell him what the rest of the world already knows. His father is a plonker.

Frankly, those three sources are the *last* places you should look to for guidance for success in business. I went on to list four of the seminal influences that affected me during my astonishing career, explaining that they came from the most un-business like places. He took copious notes, and you may wish to do the same.

Anything— ANYTHING— can be made memorable

From literature, I discovered that *anything— ANYTHING—can be made memorable.* Here I confess I am at an advantage over all of you because I possess a treasure: a collection (now out of print) of Brendan Behan's columns for the *Irish Press,* written before he published *The Quare Fellow* in the mid 1950s. If the Irish are word-millionaires, this guy was Bill Gates. Reading a few pages awakens you to the fact that *nothing* need be boring: not a memo, nor a meeting, nor a voice mail. Brendan couldn't just say goodbye to someone; it had to be 'May your shadow never grow less,' or somesuch. It needs a really positive attitude, but some companies are getting the idea. A flight attendant on Southwest Airlines now *sings* the safety announcement …

History shows us that *the difference between a mistake and a failure is the fully costed consequence.* There *is* a difference (you should fear failure, but not mistakes) but they are all mixed up in modern business. Fear, tension, and uncertainty have blurred them, and consequently we fear *both.* When you are analyzing your options, to give you some guidance, you should remember that the greatest ever failure is reputed to be the decision of the German High Command to re-commence submarine warfare one year *after* the sinking of the *Lusitania.* As a consequence, America joined World War I, and what was heading for an exhausted peace became an Allied victory—which brought reparations, the Weimar Republic, Hitler, World War II, 55 million dead, and the world on its knees. Now *that's* a failure. Compared to that, New Coke was a mistake, one that Coca-Cola quickly realized and corrected (becoming a better and more successful business as a consequence). What's the difference between a mistake and a failure in your company?

Long before it became the subject *du jour,* sport taught us that *diversity brings synergy.* Ignoring (for the moment) race, religion, gender, and sexual preference, sport showed us long ago that the harnessing of differences brings success. Most teams have a bunch of differences: small and big players, slow and fast, experienced and rookie, team players and egomaniacs, well-paid and league minimum (etc.). It's tiring and frustrating—particularly for the coach—but if/when you weld this lot together, come game time the results can be spectacular. You get much more than the sum of the parts. Now substitute those differences I mentioned at the start, and let's just get on with it.

Effective communication is what's received
Finally, our children have a lesson for us; two, in fact. They teach us that *effective communication is what's received (which is not always what's transmitted).* Furthermore, they also teach us that *some audiences receive only what they want to receive.* Both those were evident in the relationship you had with your parents, and your kids are now showing you the new improved versions. Now, if company 'communicators' digested those two simple lessons—and changed behavior accordingly—the effectiveness of business communication would be hiked by 50% overnight.

I am pleased with the last point, and consider it a rousing finish to my tutorial with William. I raise my eyes to seek permission to bow and leave, and find, to my surprise, our future monarch is fast asleep. I expect he had a very tiring day princing about the place.

At Last!
Your Questions
Answered

• •

• • • A stretch limo arrives at my house this morning, and a small arrangement of flowers is delivered to me by hand. Opening the accompanying envelope, I find, to my delight, that it is from those nice folks at the *Miami Herald*, informing me (somewhat to my surprise) that I have now been writing this column for 45 years. They suggest it would be a good time to pull together some of the most-asked questions I get, along with my wise responses. Here goes:

Q: Now that it seems to have been secured for China, do you think 'Most Favored Nation' (MFN) status could be granted to Miami?

A: *I think it is unlikely with this Administration. Congress will not accept another case with a similar record in human rights and civic corruption. I am advised, however, that—should Clinton get approval for his 'fast track' negotiation program—we may be included in future NAFTA initiatives.*

Q: In recent sporting events, when faced with *real* international competition, the US has fared badly: ice hockey (lost), Davis Cup tennis (lost), Rider Cup golf (lost), soccer World Cup (lost, but provided comic relief). How do you think the US will do in this year's baseball 'World' Series?
A: *I believe they could win it.*

Q: Are you trying to be funny?
A: *Yes and no. Measured by almost every wealth-related criteria, the US is the greatest nation on earth. But it has only 4% of the world's population, and the planet is increasingly being seen as a universal source of finance, employment, and resources as well as a universal market for goods and services. With notable exceptions (Coca-Cola, etc.), a lot of American brands are not as good as they think they are when exposed to real competition.*

Q: Do you think the current General Motors strike is playing out to a script? And, if so, where could we get a copy?
A: *Absolutely, with the final act involving plant closures that will make your eyes water. Only one copy exists, and it's in the CEO's safe.*

Q: Have you any idea what James Cameron's next disaster movie is going to be about?
A: *I understand he has acquired the rights to 'Motorola.' This tragic story tells of a magnificent company, performing wondrously, in a growing market, who hit an iceberg and within four years were splashing about in the water, miles from land with no compass. Thousands die.*

Q: How long did you laugh when Albert Dunlap got canned?
A: *Difficult to be exact. My wife timed the first phase at 2 hours 35 minutes, but then I realized that all the stockholders who followed the investment world's Mr. Bean in an attempt to create a self-fulfilling, wealth-creating, prophesy would take a bath as well.*

That added another 3 hours 12 minutes, for a total of 5 hours 47 minutes.

Q: In the recent Chrysler/Daimler Benz 'Merge Of Equals,' who got the best end of the deal?

A: *Are you serious? Every morning, Chrysler executives pinch themselves to make sure they're awake and not dreaming it.*

With notable exceptions, a lot of American brands are not as good as they think they are when exposed to real competition

Q: On a recent American Airlines flight, you noticed your 'turkey steak' had brown grill marks on it. Obviously this means that, upfront on the plane somewhere—perhaps between the pilot's cabin and the galley—there must be a jovial man, wearing an apron, flipping these steaks over an open flame broiler. Isn't this a safety risk?

A: *You would think so, but such is their dedication to making every aspect of modern commercial flight such a wondrous experience, I'm prepared to trust them.*

August 10th
Incoming! The Retro-Luddites

• •

• • • Back over in Europe, partly to enjoy the pharmaceutical industry's annual exhibition (aka the Tour de France bike race).

I also take the chance to catch up with our two sons, and over
dinner finalize the formula for the correct allocation of time between
parent and teenager when undertaking school projects. The last
one we did was definitive, and it transpires that the correct split is
for the child to spend the equivalent of his or her age in *minutes,*
while you spend the equivalent of yours in *hours.*

Thus it was that our son Ben recently spent 18 minutes on a
comparative analysis of Mary Shelley's wonderful Gothic novel

Frankenstein, comparing it with Kenneth Branagh's dreadful film version of it. I spent 50 hours on it.

I got to know the work well (did I ever), and it contains memorable words on a subject that fascinates me: the potentially damaging impact of technology on our lives. The satire was written in 1818, as the industrial revolution gathered pace. At its end, the monster's speech to the scientists ('You are my creator but I am your master') has aspects that still haunt us.

Twice in the last couple of centuries, specific *non-military* inventions have threatened society just as strongly as any weapon. Watt's steam engine, perfected around 1776, was the iron heart of the Industrial Revolution. Amidst a million other inventions, it was the one that signaled that business could become independent of nature. Within 50 years, the creation of the central factory, and the attendant use of women, children, and low-paid, unskilled labor, devastated the lives of England's ordinary families and communities.

Work for peanuts in horrendous conditions, or starve; this was the choice that summarized the benefits the steam engine brought to a nation's workforce still without voting rights, and forbidden by law to organize.

Some rebelled. The Luddite movement—which saw discarded craftsmen break into factories and smash the new machinery— threatened to delay progress, until it was itself smashed with a fury that the country rarely brought to bear, even in wartime.

The life of the artisan has never been the same since. Anywhere.

I believe history will record a second technical breakthrough as having the same traumatic social impact. It may well have a bigger one, when it has had a full couple of hundred years to run its own course.

In 1971 the microchip and microprocessor were perfected, and the outlook, this time for the white-collar worker, also changed irrevocably. Electronic data processing all but wiped out the clerical workforce. More recent developments in distributed systems

(PCs, laptops, Internet, etc.) have followed that with a massive culling of the ranks of middle-level supervision.

The irony is, of course, that this time the 'victims' can organize, and have the vote. Fat lot of good it's done; an estimated 35 million have been adversely affected in all industrial nations in less than two decades.

No Luddite rebellions this time, and it's not that surprising. This is not a warrior class. I guess folk also become anesthetized after a while, and financial compensation and enhanced welfare have provided a safety net of sorts.

This upheaval is by no means over yet— we will now move into a second generation of supervisory and administrative staff being beached

I wonder if we are right, however, to assume that this state of affairs will remain in place? This upheaval is *by no means* over yet, and we will now move into a second generation of supervisory and administrative staff being beached. The 'full' employment we read about in the US and UK is no help to them either; in fact it is largely a great big crock. Many of the new jobs are 'disposable': part-time, with lower wages, reduced benefits, fewer hours, and no security.

Can we survive *another* 35 million people being 'collateral damage' to this particular dimension of change? Because that's what is forecast, and in my view conservatively so. Something (maybe spiritual) inside me says we may yet see another Luddite movement, only this time better organized, fought differently, and with a different end.

My sympathy with these guys stems from the fact that I was born in Manchester, in the industrial north of England, and one of the cornerstones of their movement. I wonder if it will be the seedbed for the next revolution? A moment's thought, however, rules this out. Manchester's current claim to fame is that it plays host to the worst (pound for pound) soccer team on the planet (*motto: a lifetime of under-achievement*). It happens to be the one I support. If you're still in doubt, it plays in blue. Manchester has also produced a famous, if dysfunctional, rock band called *Oasis*. In addition, the weather isn't really suitable for big, open-air, revolutionary rallies:

if you can see the Pennine Hills from the city center it will rain shortly. If you can't, it's raining already. It has also been rejected more times for the Olympics than any other city, but it keeps trying. The hope is that it will eventually *irritate* the panel into agreement. At least I *think* that is the game plan.

Finally, and this is the clincher, it is the only city in the world to have been named after a breast (named *Mamucium* by the Romans in AD77: I don't believe they named it after a breast-shaped local hill; I suspect they had a vision of the future soccer team). No, it will not be the base for the Big One, the white-collar revolution. But it gave me to the world, so its place in history is secure.

September 21st
Arrivaderci Italia!

• • • *Florence, Italy:* Here, fittingly at the site of Europe's cultural Renaissance, I get first sight of my newly published book (available in the US early in 1999). European reviewers are ecstatic, with many of them noting the similarities of my prose style with that of the master—Winston Churchill. There is another uncanny link with the great man: apparently, to support his cash flow, he wrote a number of short articles in the pre-war years, for publications on both sides of the Atlantic. He was paid an enormous sum for each one. I calculate the modern equivalent to be $19,525; by an amazing coincidence this is *exactly*what the *Herald* pay me for each of these occasional pieces.

I continue my habit of calling on the head of state of any country I visit (although I still refuse all invitations from the Vatican). I have a friendly *espresso* with their dapper prime minister, who still (rather annoyingly) wants to talk about why Burger King didn't open in Italy during my golden years. The answer is at the core of the issues facing many companies as they contemplate the international development of their business.

The old formula for international development—put one of your top people in the new market as an ex-pat, and find a local company to license the distribution and/or manufacture of your product—is increasingly inadequate. All but a handful of the world's top companies now find that the only corporate architecture that works is that of a true partnership with a local company, and a partner is *much* harder to find than a licensor (or a 'brand collector' as I used to call them). It necessitates a different executive structure, with locals often filling the key roles, including chief executive (although I would always like to keep the financial controller with a direct line in to the parent). What this approach does is enable the business to *adapt its behavior* to the local market and culture more effectively than any other model—because this is the hardest challenge of all.

The old formula—put one of your top people in the new market as an ex-pat, and find a local company to license the distribution and/or manufacture of your product—is increasingly inadequate

In every country, business reflects local history, culture, society, politics, and the attitude to wealth creation. Frequently, that lot will combine in a way that Western businesses find alien, and often intolerable. For example, in most Middle Eastern countries (and many in the Far East) the glass ceiling for women is about three inches off the ground, and in many developing countries the management and compensation of the labor force seem Neanderthal to us. In a bunch of countries, the overt personal bribe is a way of business life. All these (and many, many more) are unpalatable to Western business, but they represent *their* way of doing things—and the only approach is to treat each country like a restaurant that demands you wear a necktie. In my view, you either wear a tie, or go someplace else. You do not turn up and yell and scream for them to let you in without one. It doesn't work, and it is not a class act.

The only approach is to treat each country like a restaurant that demands you wear a necktie

Italy proved an insuperable barrier for us. It is a wonderful country, full of delightful people—but it has a way of doing things all its own. It's known as the *cose d'all Italia,* and reflects that Italians have always found some impossible things easy, and some easy things impossible. Their amazing tax structure (estimated to yield 120% of GNP if it was ever all collected), their disdain for short-term returns on investment, and the need to run three sets of books all defeated us.

Of course, the passage of time and leaving Burger King have left me less jaundiced. Looking down today on glorious Florence from the nearby *colli,* there are *no* brand signs visible, and *no* fast food restaurants. Neither are missed. I was, of course, so much older then. I'm younger than that now.

But my own troubles are mounting. Back in Miami, my wife and I have a small interest in the Botticelli restaurants, and this afternoon we steal one of the master's great paintings (*Birth Of Venus c.1486*) from the Uffizi museum. The idea is to hang it in the South Miami restaurant to add to the theming and integrity. My wife (who has shown a disturbing enthusiasm for this mild felony) plans to smuggle it through Miami's customs disguised as a salami. It should be up in a couple of weeks. Do come and see it. Monday nights are usually quieter, and will offer good views.

August 31st
Albert Dunlap And Global Warming

• •

• • • I am in a good mood. I have just heard that, within 200–300 years, on account of global warming, large tracts of the county of Yorkshire in England will be under water. Now, I was born in Manchester, in the county of Lancashire, and the feud between the two counties (White Rose v. Red Rose) bears no relation to the wimpy south Floridian rivalry between Broward and Miami-Dade. Most of us see ours as a millennium-long fight to the death, and it looks like God (quite rightly) is going to side with Lancashire.

I am so happy at this news, I have decided to write *benignly* about Albert Dunlap and his canning by Sunbeam. My new, softer, position on the subject reflects that he isn't worth getting angry about. He is but a symptom of several diseases that pervade western capitalism. I've identified four.

True leaders attribute successes to the team, and only failures to themselves The first is *ego-itis*. Some time in the 1970s I was running a small chunk of a big company, and we had a good year. I wrote my year-end report, sent it in to my boss, and waited for the accolades. He called me in and threw my report back at me, telling he wanted to see a 'we' instead of every 'I.' True leaders attribute successes to the team, and only failures to themselves. I was devastated, and my ego-balloon well and truly popped, but my approach to management changed irrevocably. Now, go read Dunlap's book (*Mean Business:* Random House, 1997). The first person singular appears thirteen times on the *first* (partial) page. The CEO as a rock star isn't a new apparition (Rockefeller, Sloan, …), but whereas it works in show-biz, it is dangerous in business. Business involves complex team working, and needs many stakeholder synergies to sustain success; a single ego with a self-serving script can prove profoundly counter-productive.

Second: we have *blame-storming*. This is relatively new, reflecting the habit of many modern leaders to refuse to accept blame for anything, stalling behind lawyers, and creatively shifting the blame somewhere else. A previous generation would hold up their hands, tender their resignation and try to salvage some honor. Dunlap pleaded the 'Fawlty Tower's waiter defense' ('I know nothing, I from Barcelona'), and blamed auditors and accountants—making for an entertaining cocktail of rubbish and dishonor.

Short-termism is next, defined as 'the cooking of the corporate books to make the next quarter come in ahead of market expectations.' *Everybody* does it (trust me) because the pressures are *huge*, but in most cases it's within agreed accounting principles and pretty harmless. If it's just cutting back on the travel and entertainment budget for the last couple of months of the financial year, you're in there with everybody else, but it can get substantial and sinister. In Sunbeam's case inflating year end sales and 'creatively' using the acquisition accounting charge to support the continuing business will probably lead to a restatement of previous earnings now it's all out in the open. This stuff is way beyond the gray area.

Lastly, we have *marketmaking-itis*. This is where people in the financial community, outside the business concerned, create an artificial process whereby the stock price moves almost without reference to the inherent health of the company involved. It can happen in big companies, where the market-makers talk up a stock on the back of a Dunlap-like 'coming' together with a huge restructuring charge, which will cloud actual operating results for some time. In genesis companies, broker-dealers will do the same, restricting the stock of the early investors while they hype it in the limited market. In both cases they will exit (or short) their positions well before reality sets in, with a healthy profit. The investors outside this loop take the sure-to-arrive hit, of course.

These are the diseases that create Dunlaps, and there's no point getting upset about them because they are *fundamentals* of western capitalism and here to stay. The only defense is that it seems better than any other economic system. All we do now is just wait for the next Albert. And then we'll forget, and cheer and worship—and probably buy the stock.

These are easy challenges to deal with, of course, compared to the threat of Yorkshire drowning. Nobody should take this lightly, for, although you may be far away from it, and feel you will not be affected, you will be wrong. These guys whine and moan constantly when times are good, so you can imagine the din they'll make with water reaching their bottom lips. It will deafen the planet. One way to solve the problem, of course, would be to elect eco-friendly Al Gore as the next US President. He would, I am sure, stop global warming in its tracks. So if you vote for Al, *Yorkshire could be saved.* Wow. Now there's a powerful platform.

I'm a Brit, and I can't vote in the US,[7] and it's probably just as well.

---

7. How did that speech about taxation without representation go again?

September 7th
The Year So Far

• •

• • • As many of you are just returning from vacation, I thought I'd update you on what's been happening in the worlds of politics and business. Politics is easy: both Boris Yeltsin and Bill Clinton can now be technically classified as loopy, with the latter opting not to face his wife over the breakfast table of the first day of their 'healing' holiday. Instead, he ordered the bombing of a recent James Bond movie villain, Sheik Wellbeforeusing.[8] In the world of business:

- I'm delighted to award the 'Executive of the Year' title to AT&T's Michael Armstrong. Sure, he was working from a low base, but to land three mega-deals in his first year, as well as cutting costs by $1.6 billion and forcing executive bonuses to be performance related (wow!) shows there's still life in two

---

8. Apparently this refers to Sheik Bin Laden. The author's research let him down. Again.

old dogs (both the company and himself; he was 59 when appointed).

- 'Book of the year' goes to David Landes exhilarating *The Wealth and Poverty of Nations* (Norton, 1998). An astonishing combination of scholarship and prose, this is a *must* for anyone contemplating international business. It should be required reading for anyone with an inquiring mind.

- I'm announcing a new award, which I expect to be competed for vigorously in future. It's the American Airline's 'If You Must' award, and was born on May 31st this year, when I flew with them from Miami to London. After surviving the First Class check-in line (51 people in front of me when I joined it—I counted), I boarded the plane and asked the attendant if I could hang my suit carrier up in the closet as I had to wear it next morning. 'If you must' was the clearly irritated reply, which now sums up this Robert-Crandallized circus's all-round philosophy. In future, it will be awarded to other gems of customer-targeted aggression.

- There is a tie for the 'He's Just Not Getting It' award for the CEO who's just lost the plot. It's a tie between Boeing's Bob Ayling and Motorola's Christopher Galvin, both of whom have supervised their company's drift from world (market) dominance. The latter also won the 'PR own-foot-shoot' award outright: when *Fortune* magazine did a number on Motorola's woes, which would have troubled any existing or potential investor, Christopher was 'too busy' to respond. That moves any stock from a 'hold' to a 'sell' in my book.

- In a time of bewildering examples, the 'Earnings Multiple' of the year award goes to SAP, the 26-year-old German firm that dominates the world market for software applications that tie together and automate business processes. If my math is right, they were trading (via ADRs in the US) at *60 times* next year's *projected earnings*. For the uninitiated, that means that if the company keeps performing, and if costs, interest rates, and earnings growth remain commensurate, and if you bought the company at it's traded market value, you'd show a profit in year 62.

- The 'Titanic' award for the death of a great flagship is also shared, by Saks and Rolls Royce. Both of these 'prestige' brands were acquired by 'definitely non-prestige' branded companies during the year, proving that there is no divine right for royalty or badly run flagships.

- Biggest combined 'Ego-trip and Waste-Of-Money' goes, without challenge, to Ted Turner for the Goodwill Games. I was away in Europe when they happened. Did anybody turn up?

- The 'Sinister Threat' of the year remains that of a Chinese currency devaluation. The markets seem to be just about handling everything else (including Japanese and Russian woes), but the Chinese could blow the tent over. It's been a while since I spoke to the Chinese leadership on the subject, and I have no idea what they'll do. But I do know they'll have their own perceived interests at heart, and nobody else's.

- Result of the business world's 'Head-To-Head Gladiatorial Face Off' of the year? No question, it was in soccer's World Cup. In the final, watched by 3.5 billion people, Adidas (also known as France) beat Nike (aka Brazil). Add that to high-profile labor troubles, Michael Jordan retiring, the sneaker market tanking, and the stock price way below its previous high, and there are big question marks around the 'Swoosh.' They've a lot riding on Tiger ….

So there you have it, you're up to date.

October 5th
True Lies

• •

• • • I am the only writer on the planet yet to write about 'Zippergate,' and I fear I must correct that. But let me first tell you a couple of things I'm not going to do. You'll get no personal value judgment from me. As far as I'm concerned, its a person's right to do what he wants to lighten up those long boring phone calls with Senators. Clinton is an individual; it's his life and his script, and nothing to do with me. American individuals either voted for him or didn't, so you sort it out. I'm a Brit, and can't vote in the US. Good luck.

I'll also skip offering a point of view from the other great American vantage point; that of membership of an organized faction (you know, Congress, Senate, Southern Baptists, PTA, Teamsters, Coral Gables Beautification Committee, and so on). I've spent my life vigorously avoiding joining anything other than a soccer team, so I've no platform.

I will, however, give you some insight as to why the voices of business—individuals and organizations—have been mysteriously quiet. It's all to do with the nature of the crime. You see, nobody professes to care about Bill's sexual dalliances, the problem is that he *lied*. Therefore, we in business don't understand what the problem is, because we *all* lie. A lot.

Whoa! I can feel your outrage from here. Business people lie? Our leaders? Our *role models*? *Never*. Well, yes—they do—regularly, and without a second thought. Something happens to that pillar of integrity in the community when he or she picks up a briefcase and enters the workplace. Truth is a massive casualty.

Scott Adams (Dilbert's creator) listed the top 13 most popular business lies. Here are five of them so you'll begin to understand: *'Employees are our most valuable asset'*; *'I have an open-door policy'*; *'We reward risk takers'*; *'Your input is important to us'*; and *'Training is a high priority.'* Get the idea?

You can, of course, all add your own favorites. Mine is the one perpetrated by Big Tobacco—the biggest and longest lie in business history. Biggest because its executives have defended the safety of products that have now killed more people than Hitler and Stalin combined, and longest because they've been doing it for—what?— two generations? Libyan terrorists can only *dream* of killing the number of Americans these guys have.

You can overstate sustainable revenues, understate true costs, and misuse restructuring charges, and in some cases try all of the above

Then there are 'GAAP Lies'; in other words, those that misrepresent the financial state of your business, but that you can get away with at the year end under Generally Agreed Accounting Principles. This is easy-peasy. You can overstate sustainable revenues, understate true costs, and misuse restructuring charges, and in some cases try all of the above (which is now called the Dunlap maneuver). Behavior like this would *horrify* these upright people if their children behaved in an equivalent way.

Finally, there's a new 'fun' category available to entertain us: I call it the 'split infinitive to screw the customer' lie. It always starts, 'In order to better serve our customers ...,' and goes on with some astonishing admission of some new policy that can only *worsen* customer service. The old favorite, of course, is 'to better serve our customers we are restructuring, and 5000 staff are being laid off,' but there are some exciting and

It always starts, 'In order to better serve our customers ...,' and goes on with some astonishing admission of some new policy that can only worsen customer service

creative ones emerging. I've started to collect them, and I saw a beauty recently at my car dealership in Miami. In the maintenance and service department, there is a sign at the counter informing us that 'In order to better serve our customers' a number of things have changed, including, 'there will be no more early or late pick ups.' Well, thank you. Have a nice day.

America is rocked by the behavior of its President. We Europeans, on the other hand, have no idea what the fuss is about. Such goings on are written into the *job description* of the French President. English royalty have been doing this to *each other* for about 900 years, to the degree that their DNA is now all the same. But they've all got something to learn when it comes to plain old fashioned lying. The world of business is in a league of its own.

So, if you're taking notes I'll summarize: the male of the species can resist pretty much anything except temptation; his ability to be unfaithful is mathematically proportional to his options to be so; and business people lie a lot. If you were unaware of these facts at the start of this piece, you are profoundly wiser now.

October 19th
This Just In ...

• •

• • • *Manchester, England:* I'm in the UK to put the finishing touches to the release of the *fatwa* on Salman Rushdie. The Foreign Office insists on this as it was me who started it ten years ago with an ill-advised April Fool's joke. We all agree that enough is enough, but it was fun while it lasted.

While I'm here, I'll bring you up to date on what's happening on the British business scene. Here's the highlight reel:

- Manchester, in dark satanic north-west England, is my birth-place. During the Industrial Revolution, nearly 2000 years after it first appeared, on the back of King Cotton, coal and transport, Manchester led the world in the glories and horrors of the new economic order. Today, it proudly hosts the newest and biggest retail mall in Europe, and I visit it to sip a low-fat *latte* and watch the death throes of a once sane industry. There is no growth in aggregate consumer demand to support this kind of project (growth is coming via the direct-to-consumer channels—Internet, catalog, and home shopping). The economics, with rents rumored to be approaching $500 per square foot, are unserviceable. The 'Build it, and they will come' philosophy must now have an equal and opposite 'They've built it and our customers have gone' effect elsewhere (often on other branches of the *same* retail brands). In short, Manchester gives a portent of what will happen shortly in South Dade. You have been warned.

- Germany has a new Chancellor after 15 years (so you can be sure Poland will be keeping a close eye on the *Autobahns* for a few weeks). Herr Schröder joins Bill Clinton and the UK's Tony Blair in the 'Boomer Group' of world leaders, with their unconventional 'third way' mix of socio-economics. We wish them luck as the world circles the plughole of global recession, with little ahead (it seems) but earnings shortfalls, unserviced debts, uncovered dividends, and another 35 million lay-offs.

- Gerry Adams, of the political wing of the Irish Republican Army (IRA), and David Trimble (head of Northern Ireland's Unionists) continue their admirable and agonizing crawl along the peace process for this long-troubled island, the land of my father. In doing so, they reinforce a lesson for us all in business: when there is real impasse and division, you must be prepared to sit down and work with people you despise, or maybe even hate. It requires bravery, because progress will involve compromise, and you will not only remain hated by your opponents, but be despised by your own side as well. These qualities are rare in politicians, and even rarer in business leaders.

- Another edict from the European Legislature comes into force in the UK, defining (among other things) minimum holidays for workers. Everybody gets upset: the anti-European lobby, the *laissez-faire* philosophers, and the small business owners alike—and I'm with them. There is one element of the new legislation, however, that has my *total* support, which is a limitation of the 'mandatory' working week to 50 hours, *unless it*

The downsizing craze of the past 15 years often didn't reduce costs at all: the work still had to be done *has the written consent of the employee.* The downsizing craze of the past 15 years often didn't reduce costs at all: the work still had to be done, either by outsourcing it to contractors (often, ironically, the fired employees) and/or by forcing the residual workforce to work harder and longer (usually for no incremental reward). Of course, occasional paid overtime is attractive to workers, and having the flexibility to cover varying working patterns is essential for an employer. But the widespread modern practice of mandatory and continuous long weeks, which are now often forced on people and are quite clearly the price of keeping a job, is wrong. It simply reflects (and offsets) bad management and inadequate resourcing, and it is an obscenity of modern business life. If it takes a law to stop it, it gets my vote.

In general, all is well in my little island. In our guitar-strumming Prime Minister, Mr. Blair, we are faced with the frightening sight of a leader who parts his hair in the middle. He is also a Clinton wannabe, and Zippergate has forced us to look at our young leader in a new light. Could it happen with Tony? Has he found his own extraordinary ways to lighten those long, boring phone calls to his Cabinet? The whole of the UK is, for once, united in its view. There is not a chance. To tell the truth, we feel rather flat about it.

November 2nd
Business Travel Special!!

• •

• • • Kids are back in school. Holidays are behind us. New corporate financial years are just starting, so the Travel and Entertainment budget still exists. Hotel rooms are cheap, so there are lots of business conventions. *Yes!* 'Tis the peak time of year for business travel. To add to your excitement, here's a prize quiz on the subject:

- Your plane is scheduled to take off at 3:05 p.m. It is scheduled to arrive at 4:45 p.m. You are delayed in departing by 35 minutes. When you are in the air, the pilot announces that the flying time is 1 hour 32 minutes. When you then actually still arrive *on time*, score 10 points. *Bonus:* if you know how all this works, score 100 points.

- You are at the boarding gate for your plane, and they announce pre-boarding. When all those who need assistance, First Class, and assorted frequent flyer privilege club members have all boarded, score 10 points if there are only ten of you left. *Bonus:* If there is only you left, and you are the only one on the flight who has actually paid full fare, score 100 points.

- If you arrive late at night for your (confirmed) hotel check in, and your room (the last one allocated) is more than 17 floors high, and involves a walk past 95 other room doors, score 10 points. If it's more than 20 floors high, and past more than 100 rooms, score 25 points. *Bonus:* If it's a hotel in Indian Wells (which is where I think they filmed *The Truman Show*) and they tell you that you are in Room 'Topaz 604,' and you think, 'Wow! I must be near the elevator,' and it turns out that Topaz is an old Indian word meaning 'not actually in the same State as the hotel reception,' score 100 points.

- For your early morning jog, if you set your watch for 15 minutes for an outward run, score 10 points if you get back to the hotel in less than that time. *Bonus:* if you always beat it, on account of the fact you cheat like hell by running the first bit ever so slowly (as I always do), score 100 points.

- If you miss a plane connection by less than 5 minutes, score 10 points. *Bonus:* If (to take a random example) you are flying US Air into Charlotte to get a connection back to Miami, and you're running late with only 10 minutes to get the connection, and the pilot lands at Charlotte and announces that they've changed the landing gate and that 'we're going to have to wait a few minutes for a plane to back out of it before we can go in,' and you then *watch your Miami connecting flight back out of the gate you are waiting for and take off,* score 100 points.

- If you are on a transatlantic flight, and you go down in the ocean with (say) 2500 miles of water ahead of you and 2000 behind, and your life jacket develops one of those leaks they mention, and you have to *blow into it down one of those red tubes,* score 10 points if you then progress more than ten feet in any direction. *Bonus:* if your whistle (provided with your 'leaker' life jacket) can be heard by anybody other than the poor oiks down in the drink with you, score 100 points.

- You are on the last plane out of La Guardia to Miami. The only seat left is at the back, which you convince yourself is good because you've never heard of a plane reversing into a mountain. Everything is ready to go. Score 10 points if some plonker then boards at the last minute, with two *huge* carry-on bags, and proceeds to delay everything. *Bonus:* Sore 100 points if the guy has four *humungous* bags, of which two have to be checked at the gate, which means you lose your departure slot, are delayed 40 minutes and then line up twenty-sixth for take-off.

- You board the Avis car rental bus at the airport concourse. Score 10 if you have the driver who rented the movie *Speed* last night, and doesn't go above *or below* 40 miles per hour for the whole journey. *Bonus:* on the other hand, if the driver looks like Sandra Bullock, score 100 points.

Add up your score, and email it to me. Dinner for two at a unique Miami restaurant is the prize (unique because it is an Italian restaurant run by a Polish Argentinean married to a Dutch Slovakian).

November 16th

Houston, We Have A Problem

• •

• • • Wonderful news arrives in the mail. Fresh from their successful PR exercise in re-sending John Glenn into space to conduct his important experiments (the effect of weightlessness on denture cream), NASA have invited me to anchor their Space Station early next century. They cite my effortless communication skills (as witnessed in this organ) as the prime reason.

One of my duties will be to address the people of Earth, at dawn (GMT) on the first New Year's morning I'm up there. They say I must reflect one of mankind's great recent developments in the main theme of my speech.

I wonder if I should center on the development of the *post-industrial world* as my theme? How the great primary industries of previous generations (and my youth) have all but disappeared from the landscape of the west. How we have all become *either* movers of information or money *or* people who provide services to such people (shoes, insurance, bagels, etc.) This, of course, raises the question of what happens when those people who are still prepared to get their finger nails dirty (the Latinos, Asian Indians, Thais, etc.) no longer wish to do so. This proposal is canned by the White House as being potentially divisive, and because it could tank Nike's share price even further.

What about the less obvious one? The first faltering steps that we have taken in the *post-Christian era*. Whoa there! I can hear screams of objection already, and many of you will cite the prosperity of your own local church as evidence that this clear trend exists only in Satan's mind. But not on the world stage it doesn't, where Christianity is no longer the expanding religion. Even in America it is polarizing to have-your-credit-card-ready, hair-dyed-and-sprayed, branded evangelism or fundamentalist factions. Unthinkable as it may be, the next millennium may see the Muslim religion or the Buddhist way of life governing the bulk of the planet's spirit. Hillary (Rodders to her pals) and I decide this theme is also too contentious.

So I will talk about the *post-democracy society*. W-H-A-T? Are you *crazy*? Democracy has *won*, dammit. There are only a couple of 'commie' strongholds left, and Fidel's gotta pop his clogs soon, so that will be another one gone. This time you've gone too far, Gibbons.

Well, sure, communism has disintegrated, and most of the other regulated political systems have done or are doing so too. My concern is about what is taking their places, because I have ceased to believe that what we have, and what we feed into these places when they emerge blinking from their dark ages, is democracy.

The 100 biggest economies in the world are now split 50:50. Half of them are countries: half of them are corporations. Only *two* of the 50 countries are *not* democracies, whereas *none* of the 50 corporations are. Which would seem to blow my theory up. But my theory is that there are many more similarities between the two than there are differences, and both reflect a sort of *enlightened economic–political executive system.*

In both, an 'elected' executive team runs the show, supposedly put there by voters (in the one case) and stockholders (in the other). But in both cases the ordinary guy is so alienated and distant that they do not exercise their franchise (see recent US elections and most annual company meetings). In both cases, however, large, well resourced vested interest groups effectively control key appointments and the agenda. In both cases, if you have leverage, you can acquire control and influence—and that is *not* a democracy. And the guys without leverage have ceased to care, and the position is probably irredeemable.

The defense that, should a tyrant threaten, apathy will disappear and the people will unite to vote in the good guy doesn't hold water, either. Hitler united his people under a democracy by appealing to the wrong emotions of the public. The sad fact is that democracy is more likely 'unite' to put a nutter in rather than keep one out.

Strangely, I believe that large corporations, in their own self-interest, are becoming more responsive to a wide range of community and indirect stakeholder interests

Strangely, I believe that large corporations, in their own self-interest, are becoming more responsive to a wide range of community and indirect stakeholder interests, whereas the politicians are becoming *less* so. The only difference between the two models now is that the one that is moving in the right direction has no pretensions about being democratic.

I still have to work on the idea, but Bill signs off on this as a skeleton for the speech. Sadly, I will not be able to do my 'Castro' bit (a seven-hour, unstructured ramble) as I'll only have seven minutes to address the world. As it is I'll have to break off from my own program of vital space experiments. I will be testing, on behalf of the male of the species, and inspired by Bob Dole's terribly serious advertising campaign, erectile dysfunction under conditions of weightlessness.

Business Travel:
The Sequel!

• •

• • • It is not hard to track down when I fell out with the sciences. In the England of my youth, you took a series of public examinations when you were 16 that were designed to sort out whether you should focus on the arts or sciences. Most schools organized a trial run to make sure all the parties involved were not wasting taxpayers' money. After my 'mock' exams, a quite stunned school Principal called me into his office and informed me that I would not be sitting the proper exams in chemistry or physics. I had, apparently, broken the school record (from the wrong side) by getting a combined 7 marks out of a possible 200 in them.

Physics scored the worse of the two (3 marks), and it has fascinated me ever since. I look at a cruise ship in a port, and I know that *if I had 20 lifetimes available to me, and I spent them all learning physics, there is* no way *I would get 300,000 tons of assorted metal pieces to stand still and float.*

I feel the same way about jumbo jets and flying, and here's the frustration. These things are awe inspiring to me, and so should be the travel experiences associated with them. In fact, they are largely the opposite. In particular, business travel has become the splinter in many people's backsides as they slide down the stair-rail of their corporate mission statements.

A couple of weeks ago I wrote of a few of my own recent experiences, and structured a daft competition to see if anyone could 'beat' them. Wow—did I ever touch a nerve. Here are some extracts from the responses:

- On a plane's final approach to land, the pilot announces that he is 'going round.' Score heavy bonus points if you know what that means, and if his voice went up a *full octave*.

- Flying Miami to Milwaukee (via O'Hare) one evening, you turn up at MIA to find O'Hare is closed. You are re-routed (*big* bonus) from Miami to *Los Angeles*, and via a *red-eye* to Chicago. Then on a commuter plane to your destination.

- You check into a hotel with an antiquated phone system. You are given Room 411.[9] Big bonus points for every call to your room after midnight asking for the phone number of the local topless bar or somebody called HotChest.

- You book a car rental by phone well in advance. A price is quoted for advance payment on your credit card. You agree, then remember you can't because you will have another driver with you, who will have to produce a license, so you will have to pay at the end of the rental as normal. You are then informed the price is $60 *cheaper* than if you paid in advance. If you had paid

9. US Directory Inquiry number.

in advance you would *not* have triggered your normal discount. You may, or may not, have worked this out for yourself.

- One of your employees is on the same flight as you, and fixes to be seated next to you without your prior knowledge. Big bonus points are awarded if they want an earnest discussion on the company's Equal Opportunity Employment policy. Even more if the flight is more than five hours.

- You get to the airport *way* too early, and find there is an earlier flight to your destination. So you re-book. The early flight is then hit with a maintenance problem, and you can't get off. Your original flight takes off, and seems to dip its wings to you as it flies off. You are delayed a further three hours.

- (This is my favorite.) Check into a hotel in Boston (the person submitting this did not want to reveal the hotel brand name— only that it is run by the son of the founder, who was also called Bill). The room you have guaranteed with your credit card for late arrival has been given away, and there are no others. During the ensuing gunfight, you ask a simple question: 'If, in the event I hadn't shown up to claim my room, would my credit card have been billed?' 'Of course,' they reply. This is a big bonus earner. It is also beyond belief.

- You can make even more bonus points on this if you then drive around Boston, in larger and larger concentric circles until you reach Providence, Rhode Island, and finally find a hotel receptionist who will *bump somebody else who will then have exactly the same problem that you did.*

I could fill three columns, and—in truth—probably three thousand, on this subject. I didn't know whether to laugh or cry at the winning submission, but dinner for two awaits!

- Announcement: *'Please remain in your seats until we are finally at the gate, and the pilot has switched off the safety belt sign.'* If you have been on a plane when that announcement is made, and less than 90% of the passengers did not stand up *immediately*, award yourself a final *big* bonus.

December 14th
But Someone's Gotta Do It

• •

• • • *Hamilton Parish, Bermuda:* Here to work with some Big Business Cheeses (or *Cheesae* if you prefer Latin) on corporate internationalism.

Some folk are fascinated by the past of this place: how this group of 130 islands and reefs terrified sailors throughout history; how they were occupied by just three guys for some years; and how fortunes were made from *ambergris*, a disgusting whale secretion. Others like it for today, with its not-too-hot, not-too-cold weather, and its groomed and civilized lifestyle. Me? I kinda like it for the glimpse it gives us of the future—showing us what our supermarket prices will be like in the year 2080.

Delegates want to talk about the conventional international challenges ('Think global: act local' groan, snore). I don't. I want to talk about three things companies rarely get right when they develop their business abroad. They're not obvious, but hurt when you get them wrong.

I start with *saving the ex-pat*. These are the folk from the home country who go out on assignment, and who are often essential to success. They are domestically dysfunctional, going out there alone and/or living apart from their families and/or uprooting them all to live abroad. Sometimes all of the above. The home country attitude to them is often to treat them like Clint Eastwoods: pay them a fistful of dollars and sort out the future when it arrives. It's stupid. These people are human. As a result, they often spend more time figuring out what they'll be doing next than concentrating on the job in hand. Companies need to *stay real close* to these guys, with the lead coming from the top. That means taking time out from business issues and forcing *both* sides to talk about plotting a course for the future, including re-entry to the home country if appropriate. The corporate mortality rate for these folk is a disgrace, and it needn't be so. It is also a waste of a valuable future resource.

Next, many companies expand abroad via alliances with another company, often with disastrous results. Here's one reason. Take two western businessmen, give 'em a couple of cocktails and then draw a line on the floor between them. Their challenge is to convince the other guy to cross the line. Western businessmen (particularly men) have been known to stick it out for 36 hours, and *still* not break the impasse. Now try it with two Japanese executives. Within five minutes one is likely to say to the other: 'I'll come over your side if you'll come over to mine,' and it's all over. The difference is that western business is about *winning and losing,* whereas in the orient it is more about *both winning something.* You *cannot* go into a genuine business alliance and look to exploit it. This kind of partnership cannot be about one side winning, the other losing. It must be open, with a joint sharing of risk and reward.

You cannot go into a genuine business alliance and look to exploit it

I then confuse everybody by talking about the Elvis factor—or, rather, its avoidance. Virtually all products and services are brands

Virtually all products and services are brands today today. Your school is, so is your church. Ireland is a brand (my observation is that there are more Irish 'theme' pubs in the world today than there are Burger Kings). Elvis was, and still is, a brand. His approach to international brand development, however, was unusual: *not once* did he perform outside the US to support it. Such was the strength of the brand name, he didn't need to. You could probably put a handful of modern American brands in that same elite category—Coca-Cola, Microsoft, Ford (and so on)—but it is unlikely that lesser names can get the job done without real support from, commitment by, and the regular presence of, the brand owner. Elvis was content focusing on his 250 million domestic market; treating the rest of the world (I guess) as a bonus. It won't work today, guys. Not only will your international dreams fall short, you'll find somebody eating your domestic lunch shortly.

After 50 minutes we're all done. That's the minimum a business session can last and still justify tax exempt status for the trip in all the delegate's respective countries. As my last words die on my lips, three are killed in the rush for the exit doors. Their bodies lie untouched. By 11:00 a.m., the surviving 'delegates' have picked up their lunch boxes and are on the golf course or by the pool. I figure out what they've paid me per minute, and it's like I'm suddenly a set-up pitcher for the Dodgers.

And it came to pass that there was much joy in this small land.

December 28th
Forecasts
For 1999

• •

• • • Untouched or unsullied by extensive research, and in some cases by common sense, these are my forecasts for the last year of the millennium. Y2K, here we come:

- *January:* Inspired by the news that the French long-term unemployed have *gone on strike* (this is *true*, but, no, I don't know how it works either), the only group on earth that could claim to be more tedious, the British royal family, decide to withdraw their labor. Coincidentally, they also have nothing to strike with or against. Also, coincidentally, nobody gives a toss about them, either.

- *February:* In an exciting addition to the space-station program, Ireland launches a flat-pack, self-assembly, Irish theme pub into orbit. scheduled to dock with the station on St Patrick's night in the year 2070. The slow journey is attributed to using Guinness as rocket fuel. A gleeful Irish government spokesperson explains the goals of the project: 'We've got an Irish bar in every town on earth now, so we're after finding new markets. And, since you're asking, I'll have a pint. Thank you. May your shadow never grow less. If you insist, just a small whiskey chaser.'

- *March:* Merger mania continues. Royal Dutch Shell announces a merger with Nations Bank, but at a hastily convened afternoon press conference both companies admit a mistake. They both thought the other company was in the same business as they were. Stern faced, both CEOs promise another mega-merger for each of their companies 'at latest by tomorrow midday. And this time we'll get it right. Does anybody have a copy of the Yellow Pages?'

- *April:* Barry Gibbons' new book (*If You Want To Make God Really Laugh, Show Him Your Business Plan,* Amacom) is published to a frenzy of demand . There is open rioting in Miami as Borders run out of copies on Day 1. Pirate copies sell for thousands of dollars. The film rights are snatched up, with Harrison Ford agreeing to play Gibbons.

- *May:* European bureaucrats in Brussels, some of whom can pass wind in as many as six languages, announce a plan to 'profoundly raise the continent's sporting profile.' A plan is announced to convert The Netherlands into a super stadium. After a short feasibility study, the plan is aborted. If you include a running track around the soccer pitch, The Netherlands is not big enough.

- *June:* Worried by the lack of success of the *Mach III* razor (possibly their first ever strike-out) Warren Buffet shorts his Gillette stock. He decides to move into real estate for a period, and acquires Indonesia and Taiwan as 'rebound' opportunities, and puts New Zealand in his 401K. He takes out an option to buy Spain.

- *July:* Fresh from their success at getting Microsoft into the dock, the US Justice Department bring a case against Miami based 'Joe's' Stone Crab restaurant for uncompetitive practices. They stand accused of 'bundling:' i.e. when you buy Joe's crabs you get automatic access to their creamed spinach and nobody else's.

- *August:* After the tragic impeachment, President Al Gore (*Aaarrrgghh!*) intervenes in the drawn out NBA lock-out-cum-strike, appealing to both parties to *keep it going*. Appearing on national television, he announces that, at last, the world has found a more facile labor dispute than those involving the French long-term unemployed and the British royal family. The US must therefore defend its resulting leadership position. Mr. Gore's advisers look confused and keep handing him little handwritten notes during the broadcast.

- *September:* Motorola continues to lose share to Nokia, a company from Finland. In a nationwide survey of American business executives, when given three choices to the question 'Where or what is Finland?' 63% of respondents answered 'A form of spackling.' A further 36% answered 'a brand of golf clubs.' 1% of papers were destroyed.

- *October:* a Florida teenager, Beckie — (surname withheld) breaks the world record by inserting the word 'like' 65 times into a sentence that would otherwise contain only 12 words. Her surname is, like, withheld because she might, like, sue me.

- *November:* In a move that surprises Wall Street, Starbucks acquires Boeing. A press spokesperson for the high growth coffee business explains the logic: as Boeing have just announced (another) 50,000 layoffs, Starbucks see this move as acquiring an unlimited source of new baristas. Their stock gains 10 points.

- *December:* Celine Dion wins yet more industry awards for her soundtrack from the film of Barry Gibbon's new book. The single, taken from the multiple-platinum album, and entitled *Near, Far—My Heart Yearns For Al Dunlap,* hits the coveted Holiday number one spot.

1999

January 11th
Hot Air

• •

• • • It was a mixed holiday season for me. I started out very depressed, hearing that *Time* magazine had again overlooked me for their 'Man of the Year' in favor of a joint award for Kenneth Starr and President Teflon. Can you believe it? Just what do I have to do?

Things looked up, however, with news of a great event to celebrate in England. I jumped on a plane as soon as I heard it, and by the time I arrived, the country was already in joyous bedlam. Bonfires were burning on every hilltop, church bells were ringing, street parties were everywhere, and the Queen put on a silly paper hat to address the nation on TV. All this because Richard Branson failed (again) in his attempt to fly his hot-air balloon around the world.

I have nothing but respect for Branson as a businessman. I have written many times of my admiration of three of his specific business talents: flair, courage, and (above all) intuition. They are of the highest order, and (frankly) I wish I had more of them. But I lose the plot when folk who are successful in business decide that isn't enough, and seek populist acclaim and celebrity status in fields where their talents are not relevant. Here, they are propelled only by their egos and a wish to sign autographs. They buy sports franchises, or seek the Presidency of the US. They acquire newspapers or TV stations. They foist their views on Middle Eastern politics or Chinese human rights on anybody who will listen. They balloon (badly) half way around the world, with *huge* media coverage, as designer-intrepid explorers.

What is it with business people that they can't just do what they're paid to? Even within the framework of the business world, they stray into areas that should be left well alone. In recent years the share buyback, for example, has become a regular feature on the commercial landscape, triggered by business leaders of public companies on the assumption that the stock price of the company will benefit. This is financial engineering in its most basic form, and is *not* the function of management.

There is a strong case to be made that such buybacks actually *betray* management responsibility. Sure, their basic job is to increase earnings per share, but by *growing the earnings part*, not by restructuring the pool of available shares. Investors should determine the share price, not management. It is not hard to make the logic-leap that says you should challenge the *motives* of some of the business leaders and directors who trigger such actions. Look at how many of these companies have a CEO in his or her late fifties with a bucketful of share options, and a Board who are compensated almost entirely on stock price performance.

There is also no real proof that these schemes work: where the stock price has increased afterwards, there is usually little evidence to support the case that this wouldn't have happened anyway.

There was a time, of course, when the return of capital to shareholders was an admission of failure. That may no longer be the case, but we should view such events with profound suspicion. At the very least, I would like to see barriers introduced that prevent the business decision-makers from benefiting personally from the

If there is a case to distribute cash to the investors, do it to the proper investors, and do it as an extra-ordinary dividend

buybacks that they trigger; the alternative just stinks. If there is a case to distribute cash to the investors, do it to the proper investors, and do it as an extra-ordinary dividend. These schemes are *not* what should be occupying the time of our business leaders. They are *not* healthy, and may actually deflect management ambition and direction away from the best business mission. They may be even *less* appropriate that hot-air ballooning.

On reflection, perhaps I was too harsh in my scathing criticism of Mr. Branson. Maybe his activities are just creative (and *very* tax-effective) ways of developing a company's brand equity. Maybe, when Steve Forbes runs for President, or Larry Flint brings down a gaggle of Republican politicians, we suddenly think differently about *Forbes* and *Hustler* magazines, and alter our buying habits.

Accordingly, I have decided to stop whining and try it. Next month, flying a small biplane, towing a *huge* sign emblazoned with the name of my consultancy, I will become the first man to fly around Linda Tripp. Sponsorships will be welcome.

January 25th
Goodbye, Michael— Are You Watching, Bill?

• •

• • • So, Michael has retired. It's been a while since I met him on court. A couple of Olympics ago I was playing basketball for the English national team and we drew the US 'Dream Team' in one of the early rounds. The result was an unusual 1406–2 win for the US (Jordan 997 points), and although I had the honor of scoring both of ours, it will not go down as my finest moment. I got close enough to the great man, however, to find a reason to hate him.

My lifetime sporting idol had been Pele. In the late 1950s, as a skinny 17-year-old kid, he reinvented soccer, scoring twice in a World Cup final. For one goal, he received the ball with his back to the net, flicked it up over his head, turned, and smashed it past the goalkeeper. The poor guy marking him had to pay to get back in the stadium. I made my mind up then (I was 12 years old) that no athlete could—no, *would*—ever knock him off his perch as the greatest athlete of all time. I hated Jordan (in a weird way) because he did just that. No question.

So, if he was that good, why am I pleased to see him retire? Because he is going out at the top of his game. What a lesson he is giving to all of us generally, but to those of us in business in particular. Leave people wanting *more*. Don't hang around like wind that has been passed in a Volkswagen Beetle.

Many in business have Thatcheritis. This is a disease suffered by those who are successful, but who suddenly lose the plot. The end result is that their success is tainted in the memory by much sadder images from the end game. Margaret Thatcher became British Prime Minister in the late 1970s, taking the helm of the country at a time of abysmal economic performance and rock-bottom national self-esteem. Eight years later, to steal a business expression, there had been a turnaround. If she had done a 'Michael' then (as she would be mandated to do in the US because of the two-term limit) she would have gone down as one of the greatest peace time Prime Ministers in our history. She didn't, and the result is a much darkened legacy, with her spending her last years in power parodying herself, surrounding herself with sycophants, distancing herself from the people, and inventing mad cow disease.

It is a world where many leaders have seen their industries move beyond their intellectual and spiritual grasp, but still they hang on

Those symptoms abound in business. It is a world full of Thatchers. There are, of course, no 'limited terms' to bring a structured approach to Jordanism to the world of enterprise. When you read of a two or three year contract it's much more to do with envisaged compensation upon termination than any attempt to plan an end date. It is a world where many leaders have seen their industries move beyond their intellectual and spiritual grasp, but still they hang on. And they're tough to shift, because they have the power to surround themselves with executives (and often Boards) who have a vested interest in perpetuating the status quo.

It could be argued that Bill Gates is the Michael Jordan of the business world. If Jordan has led the NBA in personal *measurable* success criteria over the past decade, and led his team to the same *measurable* success, it could be argued that the business performance of Microsoft reflects that of the Chicago Bulls, and that of Gates reflects that of Jordan.

It's an intriguing analogy, because I think it's time for Gates to go. I think he has been the best he's gong to be for Microsoft. Increasingly, he will need the skills of a statesman—not those of a code writer and control freak—and he hasn't got them. The industry may well move away from desk-top processing towards networking from central software and databases, and that's not his best playing field. Like Jordan, however, he is a remarkable man, and he need not look on such a move as an *end*. It could be the beginning of a new challenge. Strangely, a thousand years from now, history could look back on him as the greatest philanthropist of his age if he frees up his astonishing fortune. If he stays, I see Thatcheritis on the radar screen.

But Michael has gone and a new king of the boards is needed. I wonder if I could still do it? I have inspired a movie on the subject already (*White Men* Really *Can't Jump, Especially If They Are From Manchester*), and I have a feeling that if I just had the right sneakers I could be a winner. I must ring Phil Knight of Nike (Talking of Thatcher-itis).

February 8th
Not Him Again

• •

• • • I am woken at 3:00 a.m. with the phone ringing. It's him again, forgetting the time difference between here and Baghdad.

I confess I am beginning to tire of Saddam, even though his business is very lucrative. He brings me further good news on that front: he proposes to up my monthly retainer for his US Public Relations business to an astonishing $55,000. But he wants better results: more sound bites, photo-ops, and a slot on the *Daily Show*. He wants me to push his image as a tough but fair statesman, a family man, a man who achieves goals against great odds, and a man who only *occasionally* beheads those who tick him off. In short, he wants to be the Iraqi Bill Parcells. He gives me a week to come up with a plan.

The *big* story of the National Football League this season, irrespective of the Super Bowl result, is yet another 'turnaround' from Parcells. Following the miracles he performed with the Giants, and his even more remarkable achievements with the Patriots, the turnaround in the fortunes of the Jets has given him instant legend status. He seems to do it with the same formula each time. He is a self-confessed Nasty; a control freak. His approach to people management seems to be that they can only deliver under constant supervision and when cornered like rats in a trap. The people around and him are intimidated. There is much 'collateral damage,' but the results always come.

Those of us in business should ask two questions. First, are there lessons for us in how he achieves his goals? Second, does it have to be done that way?

Here's where I need to look in the mirror, for my reputation was once in turnarounds (see the cover of *Fortune* magazine in April 1937). Do I see a Parcells looking back at me? There is, of course, one obvious physical difference between us: one of us has kept his boyish good looks, while the other has degenerated into a fat pig (our attorneys have asked that you work this out for yourselves). But, apart from that, the sad news is we have things in common.

For a turnaround, the leader must first have a crystal clear idea of two or three things that are needed. The bad news for him or her is that they may not be what the common audience thinks is wanted, but you cannot be deflected. It is not about being popular. It may be boring, unglamorous, and unpopular, but that's water off a duck's back to these guys. The press and the fans want some sexy offensive free agents. Parcells sees the need for a center.

Second, bring your own people into key areas. There are innocent victims, and many see it as just change for change's sake, but you can't do the whole thing on your own. Put a couple of 'Centurions' in parts of the business that you know they can handle, and that you can then forget about while you concentrate on the other bits. In 1989, Burger King's supply chain was a disaster, so I brought a supply chain genius in who had worked with me before (Chris Dams). Then I forgot about it. Within four years it was the best in the industry.

So, I'm two for two with Parcell's formula so far, but here's where I differ. You must have some faith. You cannot take every decision

You must have some faith—you cannot take every decision and you cannot control every tenet of the business and you cannot control every tenet of the business. If you are going to put your own people in, if they are not of the quality that enables you to trust them to do the job, then I believe you are merely substituting a different longer term set of problems for a solutions to a short-term set. There *are* other ways to do it, and Messrs. Gerstner (IBM), Armstrong (AT&T), and Jobs (Apple) have achieved spectacular turnaround results using a more nutritional mix of Machievelli and Pat Boone.

By now, I have my response for Saddam, and it is infallible. If he wants public acceptance in the US, I tell him he must adapt a five-point plan. I email him the details immediately. He must first have a sexual relationship with an intern in his palace, *but not have sex by his definition*. Then let Alan Greenspan and the guys at the US Treasury run his economy as well. Then have a hostile Congress that stops him spending dumb public money. Then be photographed (wearing safety glasses) nailing some wooden beams in a house in the Kurdish Projects. And, finally, re-name his daughter after an English soccer team. Within weeks, this formula guarantees an approval rating in the 60–70% range.

February 22nd
Restlessness Wins

• •

• • • I have, several times in the past, taken the opportunity of cleansing my inner body in the early months of the year. 1999 is no exception, and I find myself in Europe for a 30-day Irish diet, during which time I consume nothing but Gaelic coffee. At first sight this mixture of coffee and Irish whiskey may seem, to many of you, a tad incongruous. But the substance in question is unique, in that contains all the essential food groups for the male of the species: caffeine, alcohol, fat, and sugar. If you sprinkle salt on it, it is perfect.

While on these shores I will pass on my observations on the struggles of Marks & Spencer, until recently England's premier retailer. They are little known in the US, apart from being the low-profile owner of Brooks Brothers, but their current plight can give us all an indication of the increasingly bizarre management talents needed to survive and prosper in business today.

Marks and Sparks (as they are universally known) built their success on a strange mixture, which I suspect they stumbled on by accident. Originally a textile retailer, with their own brand name (St. Michael), they pressurized their (mainly English) suppliers in to giving them a distinct blend of price and quality that proved just right for Middle England. They then expanded—brilliantly—into value-added food, and later added furnishings and other stuff. They further pressured their suppliers (on quality and price) by offering a no-questions-asked returns policy to their customers. As a result of this, they decided not to provide customer dressing rooms for their clothing sections.

They pioneered an in-house credit card and, again as a direct result, refused to accept others. They held firm with their policy of (largely) British supply, emphasizing it as part of their market distinction. Put all that together, and mix in some of the country's best retail locations and the result was nearly two decades of market dominance, superb business performance, and stellar stock price gains. Their leader, Sir Richard Greenbury, reached demi-god status.

Then things changed, and their very strengths suddenly started giving off different images. Middle England woke up to the attraction of producer (i.e. non-retailer) textile brands like Hilfiger and GAP, and buying the St. Michael brand label was suddenly like kissing your sister. Globalization brought cheaper foreign sourcing, and when they tried to switch from British sourcing they created a real stink. No major credit cards? No customer changing rooms? Done for all the right reasons a decade ago these positions suddenly looked arrogant. All *that* lot came together in about a single year, and suddenly market share was down, profits tanked, the stock price hit an iceberg, and everybody was a Monday morning quarterback. It all seemed so obvious. Sir Richard was a donkey after all.

Thousands of essays have been written on the essential skills of business leadership. Many advocate passion, others say charisma, or vision, intellect, interpersonal skills, communicating skills, and so on. The Marks and Sparks 1998 story firms up in my mind an idea on the subject I've been toying with for a while. *The* essential skill is none of the above; it's *restlessness*. It's the complete inability to ever be comfortable. It's the insistence that you look on your business *every* day as though you'd landed from Mars.

The essential skill is none of the above—it's restlessness: the complete inability to ever be comfortable

How would you go about doing what you do if you were from another planet? If it's different from what you do, change, or you're in trouble. If it's not bust, *break* it. If you feel good, *something's wrong*. Life isn't just about doing something better, faster, cheaper. It may be about doing something entirely different. In my observation, all the Big Winners in modern business executives have it. Interestingly, few 'modern' politicians do; it is not an obvious strength of Al Gore or the Bush Brothers (groan, snore).

It's about a mind-set. While in the UK, I witness a daft competition: to find the best *question* that will provide the answer 'Yes, we have no bananas.' The wonderful, wonderful, winner was: '*Waiter! Is this a* cucumber *split down the middle, surrounding two scoops of ice cream, with whipped cream, flaked almonds and cocktail cherries on top?*' Now, just pause and reflect. If you could find the person who came up with *that* answer, you will have found a mind that could reposition Marks and Sparks at the top, and keep them there.

You will *not* have found a mind you would want in the White House or Downing Street. What a sad planet.

6th March 1999

The Lords Of Misrule

• •

• • • I am lucky to have homes in two places: near Miami, and in a small English market-town called Ampthill. I have decided to lead one of them in an application for the 2008 summer Olympics, but cannot choose which one.

If the choice is difficult, the application will be easy. I have earmarked a key (male) official from the International Olympic Committee (IOC), and an old friend of mine (Madame Fifi de la Poltergeist) has agreed to deliver the application personally. She will ask only 40 minutes of his time, in a private one-to-one situation. We will then provide a couple of scholarships at Oxford University, and a small token of our gratitude; say a $1,750,000 voucher for Harrods. That should do the trick.

While Juan Antonio ('just call me Your Excellency') Samaranch continues his obscene rule over the corrupt body that supposedly governs the planet's sporting virtue, he finds he has a rival. In Strasbourg, The European Union's equally arrogant and unaccountable Executive, led by Jacques Santer, is reeling from disclosures of corruption and mismanagement. Some $10 billion has 'gone astray,' and accusations of pork-barreling and personal expense abuse are rampant. Typical of those in the firing line is Edith Cresson, one of the few people on earth to combine (and fail at) being female and an elected head of state (France). She has been put out to grass in the EU and, by all accounts, makes the IOC guys look amateurs.

In my observation, these people are the lowest in the food chain. I write little of President Clinton's 'impeachment' because it's none of my business, but I have a view as to why he remains popular. His real crime was being found out, whereas other Presidents weren't. Once he was scrambling about unprotected, he ducked and dived, bluffed and blustered, and, yes, lied, to protect (primarily) himself. His approval ratings hit 60–70%. That is because 60–70% of men would do exactly the same. It is also because 60–70% of women *know* that 60–70% of men would do exactly the same. Now, compare that 'crime' to the obscenities of Santer and Samaranch and their cronies, with their premeditated abuse of power for personal gain, and you know why the wise US people have salvaged a sensible solution for Clinton despite their elected representatives. A veteran post-war British politician, George Brown, had a fine name for the likes of Santer and Samaranch. He called them the 'Lords Of Misrule.'

Whereas I see sport and politics recruiting daily to the ranks of the Lords Of Misrule, I see business slowly cleaning up its act

So, what's this to do with business? For once I am going to praise the crazy world of Dilbert,[10] downsizing, and diversity workshops. Whereas I see sport and politics recruiting daily to the ranks of the Lords Of Misrule, I see business slowly cleaning up its act. It is still widespread, and it will never be clear from of the abuse of power for personal gain, but many corporations have now implemented strong policies and

---

10. Are you old enough to remember when Dilbert was funny?

procedures that effectively govern ethical behavior in business. It was needed.

In 1992, when still just a couple of years into my time on the bridge at Burger King, I was approached by a major vendor. His proposal was to fly my wife and me out to the Barcelona Olympics, put us up on a yacht, and helicopter us in to whichever event we fancied— every day for two weeks. He was stunned when I asked him to calculate the cost of this exercise and knock it off the price of his product instead. Then a lot of other people in the company (and the system) were also stunned when we used this as an example to rake out a lot more of this crud. I'm not deaf, dumb, and blind; I know a lot goes on. But it is getting better in business, and the trend is in the right direction. So, score one for us for a change.

I have now made my mind up, and decided to plump for Ampthill for the 2008 Olympics. The attractions of Miami are truly powerful (15 unused stadiums, etc.), but they are as nothing compared to the magnificent pulling power of Ampthill's great TV-friendly sporting facility. This is the Diana, Princess Of Wales, Memorial Games Room, situated over my garage. In it is a pool table, dart board, and a rowing machine. The *pièce de résistance*, however, is a wondrous 1960s juke box full of collections of the 'Greatest Hits' of artists who mostly died choking on their own vomit.

March 23rd
I'm Dr. Jekyll
AND Mr. Hyde.
Get Used To It

• •

• • • Hello. Allow me to introduce myself. I buy the goods and services of American and British brand owners. I am a *customer*. My name is Dr. Jekyll. It is also Mr. Hyde.

Let me tell you how this works, Mr. Brand Owner, because you are just not getting it, and you need to if you are to survive and prosper.

Recently, I stayed overnight in two separate, very expensive, American branded hotels (courtesy of somebody else paying). Staying in a hotel is a unique customer experience, because there are (literally) thousands of dimensions to the product and service you buy: from the welcome at check-in to the comfort of the pillows; from the position of the room phone, to the free shampoo, and so on.

Experience #1: I arrived *very* late, having had what we now call an 'American Airlines' day. I got a real friendly welcome. The room was just fine. I slept well. In the morning, I worked out, in great facilities. Everything was just dandy, and I was actually enjoying my experience. I got ready to go to my meeting, and discovered I had forgotten my razor. I phoned the front desk to see if they had what I call an 'Alzheimer's Box,' i.e. a supply of spare disposable razors, tooth brushes, etc. for aging, forgetful guys like me. They had. Isn't this a great place? I went down to the front desk, and got one from a smiling receptionist. *And then she charged me 95 cents for it.* Something imploded in me, and all that good stuff was flushed away. I spent the rest of my stay there muttering to myself, frequently repeating the words 'parsimonious bastards.' I determined I would never stay with that brand again, ever, anywhere.

Experience #2: Same thing. However, if the first hotel was hugely expensive, this one was *HUGELY* expensive. I got a great welcome, and a lovely room. I slept well. Great work-out facilities. I was up early as I was on West Coast time. (In Palm Springs, average age: 109. I believe they filmed *The Truman Show* movie there.) At 6:00 a.m. I went to the lobby for a coffee out of the 'early morning' urn that most hotels provide these days. Great news! It was there, waiting, all ready and hot—*together with a guy who charged me $2.95 for a cup of regular filter coffee.* I was in such a state of shock, I tipped him. You see, after years in Burger King, I know how much that cup of coffee cost the hotel. It works out at (approximately) $0.000,000,72 per bathtub-full. I imploded again. All over the lobby. Messy business.

Study after study shows that modern customer loyalty does not come from just being satisfied, or even being very satisfied, but only from being completely satisfied

These are extreme examples of what is going on in the market place, where brands run by idiots are losing loyalty to brands that are not. Study after study now is showing that modern customer loyalty does not come from just being satisfied, or even being very satisfied, but only from being completely satisfied. Not *one* dimension can go wrong.

These two hotels took me in, and held me as Dr. Jekyll for most of my stay. They spent a lot of money doing that, and charged a lot (more) back from me in return. That's part of the deal in these places; value is not always price driven. If you want a confession from me, it is this: I would not have known, or cared, if they had charged 50 dollars more for the two nights.

So, a genius turned Dr. Jekyll into Mr. Hyde by getting me to spend the combined, additional, mighty total of $3.90 (remember, in reality the combined *cost* to the hotels of the coffee and razor was infinitesimal). Who is it, in these places, with an IQ level that indicates he needs watering every day (it is a man, trust me), who insists the coffee urn and Alzheimers Box are treated as *profit centers* instead of *service centers*? Why, *why*, would somebody be happy at gaining four bucks, but losing me for *life*? And this after I've had a 99% great experience? You know, you just know, don't you, that there are accountants involved.

Of course you must make a profit in business, and all customers expect value. But there is no law that states that either of those has to be incompatible with shaping a total experience that will bring the customer back again and again, because that loyalty is the surest way to survival and prosperity. It is one of the few ways to get a sustainable competitive advantage today. And, still, they don't get it.

Now, if you think I'm unreasonable in hotels, you just want to see me in an Irish theme pub.

April 5th
The Year
So Far ...

- McDonald's trip up again. In January, the Golden Arches offered a two-for-one promotion, backed with advertising. They promptly ran out of product, and alienated franchisees and customers alike. Of course I have an ego (I'm male), and I like to think my team played a role in the 1990s' turnaround of Burger King. However, we shouldn't underestimate McDonald's' incompetence in the mix of our success. I still laugh when I think of the McRib. I think the idea was that my mouth should water at the thought of it; not my eyes. And then there was the McLean. With added seaweed. Stop. *Stop!* It's hurting! Where are the tissues?

- 1999 sees us introduced to the *sick-out*. This is the tactic used by American Airlines' pilots to effect a strike without having the courage to break their contract. Now we have this tedious airline, already managed by incompetents, piloted by obnoxious greedsters. There have been many noble fights against the excesses of capitalism in history. Many exist today, and new ones will occur. Nobody should confuse this dispute with any of them. This is simply a bunch of life's winners defending their indolence. They target defenseless consumers by leveraging their monopoly power at a time when it will create most inconvenience. And they leave their colleagues— those valiant people handling check-in desks and service counters—to take the flak. Nice touch, guys.

- *Aftermath of Clinton:* I get an unsolicited speech over the shoulder of a cab driver. How is he going to explain all this 'Monica' stuff to his grandchildren? I suggest (it has been a long day) that he asks his grandchildren to explain it to him, and we finish the journey in silence. As a philosopher, I would make a good plumber, but there may be something in this throwaway remark of mine. We Boomers have lost the plot. Our children are not much better, but the next generation is tuned right in. They can operate the VCR, they use *all* their fingers on the computer keyboard, they know what the right-hand clicker is for on the mouse, and they are at ease with the new morality (just like we were in the 1960s, remember?). 'Hey, Gramps—nobody got killed, it was only sex, everybody knows about BJs, everybody lies. Let's just, like, chuckle and move on. It's a really cool world you've left us. OK?' It also occurs to me that this double generation gap is alive and well in business. Boomers didn't understand Dilbert, even during the period when it was funny.

- *Best wrong excuse of the year:* Boeing blaming Asian economic woes for its current underperformance. Rubbish. That's just a convenient way of deflecting the truth. Nobody is fooled, let alone the eagle eyes of the research team for this column (both of them). Boeing has been out-manouvered in world markets by the European Air Bus. Period. and it will get worse.

- How did Nordic Track mess up so badly? They had great products in a booming market. That's a cool formula, and you've got to try hard to bollix it up. Their case study should be essential reading for those riding high now, like Hilfiger and Nokia. Pity Levi Strauss couldn't get to study it in time.

- Would you buy anything from Laura Ashley? Neither would I. I guess if I had a 107-year-old aunt, and she specifically asked that I design the room in which she would be 'laid out' immediately after her death, I might go to them for some wallpaper. I spy a lost cause.

- Did nobody see Boston Chicken's (aka Boston Market's) troubles coming? That's what happens when you concentrate on making money by puffing up the share price when you should be concentrating on selling great food. See also Planet Hollywood and Kenny Rogers.

- *Book of the year:* I've just caught up with one published in 1997: *The History Of Money* by Jack Weatherford (Three Rivers Press). We've been using physical money for more than 25 centuries and are about to stop. The history is fascinating; how the development of money followed civilization, and occasionally vice versa. Money is now more god-like than ever (totally abstract and without corporeal body). Overall this book is a great reminder of how ugly we can be as a race.

Money is now more god-like than ever (totally abstract and without corporeal body)

- My old flame Madeleine (Albright) calls me at home in the early hours. The bombing of Yugoslavia is to begin, largely with US munitions. The telephone line is bad and I am confused. I assume this to be a worrying escalation of the Banana Wars, previously limited to the whining self-interest of the paid lobbyists of Chiquita and Fyffes. Bombing indeed. This must stop, and I will make appropriate calls shortly.

Anyone For Tennis? Or Start-Ups?

• •

• • • I have a soft spot for the Davis Cup, the international tennis tournament. It's been more than half a century since we Brits won it, but I remember it as if it were yesterday. Fred Perry and I won the deciding doubles match on a balmy spring Saturday in the late 1930s, and all was well with the world. My body was bathed in sweat from wearing my long white flannel pants, and my arm exhausted from thundering down 125 mph serves with my wooden racquet, but I felt good.

I watched this years tie—Britain v. the US—with interest. By dint of cheating (one of our players is Canadian; the other was born with a tennis court in his back yard) we fielded a team containing two of the world's best players. The US, however, was without its two big stars. These poseurs (Agassi and Sampras) decided that they had priorities other than representing their country, and it was left to a (now) lowly ranked tour veteran, Jim Courier, to answer the call for the Stars and Stripes. And it came to pass that he did just that.

On a fast surface picked to favor us, with a hostile British crowd howling him down, Courier beat both of our younger, higher-ranked guys in two marathon matches. He simply ground them down, and 'out-hearted' them. It was magnificent stuff.

I'm a mixed bag of patriotic emotions now. I was born English, we have a home there, and there is much I still like about the old place. But, frankly, I no longer give a monkey's about our politics, parliament, and tedious royal family. In truth, much of our history is nothing to be proud of, and many of our traditions are fatuous. If I open my wallet and pay for my beer with a euro instead of a pound, it tastes the same. If Wales, Scotland, and Ireland (please!) want to play at being proper countries, I'll hold their coats. But when it comes to sport, I'm a fanatic and (frequently) an embarrassment. If England are playing anybody, at any sport, I'm a basket case. Every vein in my body is at risk. And there I was, rooting for a Yank against our guys.

It's his attitude I love. It's more than just a will to win, it's a refusal to even contemplate losing. It's more than just determination; it's a mixture of surging adrenaline, bloody-mindedness, illogical self-belief and three teaspoons of barking madness. It is a rare talent. It is not sustainable for long periods. And it has its place in achieving success in business as well as sports.

Surprisingly, I do not believe it is a talent best deployed—or even essential—in leadership in large corporations. The 'must-have' ingredient in the skill mix for these folk is a kind of restlessness, a distaste for comfort and a continual (daily) challenge of the status quo. In itself, that is a rare talent, but it is a different one than the 'Courier' Factor.

Where the latter has its impact is at the other end of the business spectrum, in the genesis company. Business start-ups are the life blood of capitalism, but their failure rate is staggering: well over 90%. The rewards for success, of course, are potentially astronomic, which is why thousands of them start chasing the impossible dream every day.

My observation is that it is not the actual product of the new company that is the determining factor in its success, but the Courier Factor possessed by the entrepreneur. The barriers to winning at this game are mountainous. Not only do you have to develop, source, market, and sell your product, but you also have to navigate through the shysters and ne'er-do-wells who seek to 'help' you with early financing. You do this (usually) with your house over-mortgaged. You use one credit card to pay another. You can't afford quality people to help. Taxation and regulatory authorities cramp your every move. Banks won't lend you money till you can prove you can afford not to borrow it. Add it all up, and every day looks impossible. Astonishingly, however, where sane people would see no hope, you see no problem. The Courier Factor—plain vanilla resilience—becomes key. As an entrepreneur, you might not win with it, but you will not win without it.

My observation is that it is not the actual product of the new company that is the determining factor in its success

Enjoy your Davis Cup triumph while it lasts, America. We'll have you next year. If Courier can do it, so can I. I'm making a comeback. That's if I can still get in my long white flannels. And I may need to borrow a sports bra.

May 3rd

Capitalism:
The Good, The
Bad, And The Ugly

● ●

● ● ● In March this year, in a piece called *Lords Of Misrule*, I ripped into both the International Olympic Commission, and the Executive of the European Union, for their widespread malpractice. Within two weeks, several members of the IOC had 'resigned,' followed by all 22 European Commissioners.

Clearly, this column is now essential reading for all heads of state, senior worldwide elected representatives, appropriate royalty, media moguls, and all international religious, educational, and business leaders. Such responsibility, and I must take it seriously. It is with a heavy heart, therefore, that I announce that I have decided to bring down the British government.

The British Trade and Industry Secretary, whose first name is Stephen, which should worry us enough, has announced his intention to meddle in the market forces that have created one symptom of modern capitalism: the super salaries of 'fat cat' businessmen. Smelling cheap votes, he's prattling on about capping them—somehow. He hasn't come up with a plan yet. Fathead. This man should not be allowed to breed.

Of course it is obnoxious that someone picks up 300–400 times more reward than another when they both work for the same corporation. Sure, it's abhorrent that Jerry Seinfeld earns zillions when there are soup kitchens in Washington DC. Yes, it's ludicrous when Kevin Brown, a socially impaired baseball pitcher, signs a *nine*-figure deal with a baseball team when nurses and teachers wouldn't earn that in 50 lifetimes. And whatever Don King makes, it is *way* too much. But these stomach-churning anomalies are *part* of an overall good-news picture. We interfere with them at our peril.

Capitalism works, as does freedom— everything else sucks

Capitalism works, as does freedom. Everything else sucks—we know that now. But we pay a price for it. We have to let people burn our flags, say things we don't want to hear, and occasionally strike a free-market price for the selling and buying of goods and services that stinks in the eyes of most of us. But every time we try and interfere, we get it wrong. *Capitalism never has been about equality*, but we should applaud its strengths, not decry its weaknesses.

While we're at it, lets get a few more nasties out of the way. Not only is capitalism inequitable, but it is also exploitative. David Ricardo's 'Iron Law Of Wages,' written around the end of the eighteenth century sounds ugly: *'wages are the price which is necessary to enable labor to subsist and to perpetuate their race, without either increase or diminution.'* Well, we've progressed a long way from there, haven't we? Haven't we? My observation is that, if you fancy that quote up with a bit of HR-speak, and omit the last 10 words, you have the philosophy driving most modern programs of re-engineering and virtually all of today's mega-mergers. But the paradox continues, because exploitation is also OK. When you add it all up, there is more wealth created and distributed to more people under capitalism than there would or could be under any other system.

I'm on a roll now. Not only is it inequitable and exploitative, capitalism is also destructive. From the lives of over-worked children in the third world, to the rainforests and strip-mined landscapes. From the hideous brand signs cluttering western suburbs and highways, to filthy rivers. From Chernobyl to Three Mile Island. All these are just different dimensions of the price we pay for entry into this wondrous club, which somehow manages to learn from most of its mistakes and keeps getting better. Slowly.

Finally, capitalism is about winning and losing—this, of course, is a bummer only if you are in the losing camp

Finally, capitalism is about winning and losing. This, of course, is a bummer only if you are in the losing camp. The system thrives on competition. Companies beat other companies, products beat other products, and people beat other people. The winners celebrate, and sometimes gloat. The losers often die or disappear, and there are wakes, funerals, and tears. But, as Darwin once daringly convinced us, it is actually the key to overall survival.

Inequitable, exploitative, destructive, and Darwinistic. Man, it can be ugly—but it works and it's all we've got. And it's given the west a golden age, for never has the quality of life been so high for so many for so long. So, let's stop whining and raise a glass.

I must stop now as I have Tony Blair on hold. Our Prime Minister with the Middle Hair Parting. He's got wind of my plans, and has offered me a knighthood if I'll let his government stay in office. Hmm. I can't usually be bought, but ... *Sir* Barry? What do you think? It could get me a table in Botticelli's Trattoria on a busy Friday evening.

Mama Said There'd Be Days Like This

• •

• • • A dreadful day. At 5:00 a.m., the 'incoming' siren in my video conferencing suite (between my gymnasium and dressing room) goes off. It is Rupert 'Digger' Murdoch, the head of News International, calling from Australia, and he is furious. News has just reached him that it was my intervention, with a few well-placed phone calls, that caused the British government to block his company's acquisition of Manchester United. Arguably the world's biggest soccer club (or 'branded product' as he calls it), this would have been added to his collection of two of the UK's national newspapers and our only satellite TV system. All this, of course, would be added to his US ownership of Fox TV, the LA Dodgers and many—*many*—other assets in the world of media and entertainment.

My position on government intervention in business is clear: the market if possible, the state if absolutely necessary

My position on government intervention in business is clear: *the market if possible, the state if absolutely necessary.* This man, however, is on track to own everything we watch, read, and, ultimately, think. As I peer at my screen, I believe I can see spittle forming at the corners of his mouth, he is so angry. But I am resolute. The Digger must be stopped. I'm doing my bit. I can only hope you are.

Luncheon is with Dan Quayle. This is the result of a shadowy group of people approaching my Beijing offices,[11] and retaining me (lucratively) to interview all the candidates for next year's US presidential election. Fresh from their success with the Democrats, they want to know who to put their money behind next. The interview is just awful. I have to drink to get through it, and before we finish I am surprised to find I have consumed 28 vodkas, a carafe of fresh prune juice, and a whole bottle of champagne. Our talk is punctuated by long silences. Sometimes he just can't find the right word. Sometimes I just stare at him and wonder how he beat the other million sperm to get here in the first place. We agree his only chance is a 'Back To Nature/Ecology' ticket. In an inspired moment we pledge to follow Pamela Anderson's magnificent example, and have our own breast implants removed.

When I type my afternoon report (a bit shakily) to my Chinese masters, I tell them to leave their money in the bank. It is a waste of time trying to buy US politicians; they cannot influence anything more. Big companies today might have their investors in Europe, production in Taiwan, vendors in Brazil, and markets in California. If any government threatens on any front, they just move all that around a bit. Governments are also impotent. Sure, they can insist on your burger label telling you how much sodium you are about to eat, but the *big* stuff, like the production and sale of guns and tobacco, whose products kill more voters each year than, say, a reasonably sized world war, proceed largely unhindered.

---

11. Situated in the newly completed Gibbons Tower; the world's highest skyscraper at 3756 feet tall. I know where the future lies …

Dinner is with beleaguered Doug Ivester, the recently appointed head of Coca-Cola; the poor guy who had to follow the serene and *hugely* successful Roberto Goizueta. I have a headache, and can't face food. I need coffee, and insist we hit the best Starbucks in Miami (UM campus), where Doug introduces me to a 'Red Eye:' a triple shot of espresso in a coke. He is not happy. Since his appointment, Coca-Cola's stock has underperformed the market by 17%, sales and earnings are poor, and the market value of this icon has just been hilariously overtaken by America Online.

I tell him to lighten up. These things happen in cycles. McDonald's' success in the late 1980s was not because they were good; it was because Burger King was a crock. I fear much of Coca-Cola's success in the 1990s was for the same reason; i.e. their key competitor (Pepsi) was dreadful. What happened in both cases was that when the ailing competitor woke up, as Pepsi has done recently, the *numero uno* found it wasn't as good as its figures had been indicating. It is then forced to do some overdue, radical stuff. That is his challenge.

We have a couple more Red Eyes each, and I leave. In parting, I tell him that he must become the lowest cost producer, get his marketing relevant again, and drive massive new distribution. He should then come back and see me in two years.[12]

I crawl into bed, exhausted, but cannot sleep. It may be the weight of such responsibilities. Or it may, of course, be the effects of nine espressos.

---

12. Doug has asked me to footnote the information that everything in this is technically correct apart from the fact he wasn't actually present. If you're picky for that kind of detail, I suppose I'd better mention it...

Thanks For The Memories

• •

• • • Behind every successful man there is an astonished mother-in-law. Behind everyone who succeeds in business, there is an astonished banker.

When I quit Big Business to do My Own Thing (i.e. sleep late), most wished me well and thought they understood. My bank manager didn't. He thought I was depriving a village somewhere of an idiot. He asked me for my reasoning. I didn't have any available. Better late than never, I've observed a few things recently that have helped explain why I was fed up.

Let me first raise my glass to Andrea O'Neill, the British Airways stewardess who lost a bet with her colleagues about their plane's arrival time at Genoa airport. She paid up immediately, by running around the plane on the tarmac, wearing only her panties and a life-jacket. The London tabloids got hold of it and there followed the usual sanctimonious humbug from the PC police: what's the world coming to, disgusting example, our poor children, didn't happen in my day, she should be fired, omygod, blah, blah, blah. (Oh! By the way, on page 3 there's a full page color photograph of a supermodel showing what she might have looked like, and on page 9 there is an in-depth article on sexually depraved bets throughout history ... with amazing pictures ...)

What happened was that BA (amazingly) treated it with the light hand it deserved, and the world smiled. And I fell into a nostalgia-warp for the days when people occasionally did *daft* things in business, and they brightened up the days. Today, daft things are almost unheard of, and smiling itself (like smoking) will shortly be banned from inside business premises.

Then I read that Mexico proposes to abandon the three-hour lunch, in an attempt to modernize and globalize it's approach to business. Somebody should tell Mexico that lunch is not their Big Problem. Still, I was aghast. As a Brit, I am no fan of the French, believing that country to be an excellent candidate for the neutron bomb (keep the buildings, countryside, wine, food, and cheese, but get rid of the people[13]). The sad fact, however, is that the French are now the last bastion on earth of the proper luncheon. They deserve credit. Ouch. That hurt me to say that.

I miss those occasional lunches, and they are the buffalo of business—all but wiped out. My Dutch business colleague is illustrative of the exciting new approach to the workplace, bringing rice cakes to munch during his eight-minute lunchtime. He looks increasingly like Keith Richards. You have all been warned.

Now for the stuff that heroines are made of. Dr. Heather Clark saved the life of a guy with a blood clot on his heart, by performing open-heart surgery on him *on the floor of a British pub*. Respond-

---

13. Apart from my nephew's French family, who are wonderful. All of you. It is important you understand that. Really important. Jesus, that was close. I thank you, Lord, for the invention of footnotes.

ing to the sudden emergency (the man had collapsed and technically died) she used a pair of scissors to cut through his breast bone and lifted the rib cage to remove the clot. The dead heart started to beat again. Some drinkers held some lights to help, others carried on watching the TV soccer. I would have fainted. The 'patient' is now home and expected to make a full recovery.

What's all this to do with what eventually drove me away from Big Business? This woman should have a statue cast in her honor. Not only was she skilled and confident enough: she *took the risk* without a moment's thought. My observation is that in the US (and increasingly in the UK) capable people happening on such a scene would *not* attempt the impossible with a pair of scissors. Why? If it went wrong, they would surely be sued.

Attorneys are now taking the majority of substantive business decisions, following their creed of 'least exposure'

When I joined Big Business 30 years ago, if you wanted two words to substitute for management, they would have been *risk taking*. Today, the same exercise would produce the words *risk avoidance*. Attorneys are now taking the majority of substantive business decisions, following their creed of 'least exposure.' The spirit of Heather Clark has all but gone.

That's what I missed: daft people, occasional long lunches, and taking risks—and quit. You can have what's left and are welcome to it. The way things are going, I may have to start writing this column myself.

Paperback
Writer

• •

• • • Another trip to the UK to help Prince Edward write his speech for his upcoming nuptials. It is no coincidence that I am there on the morning that the Palace announce the appointment of the new *Poet Laureate,* as I am advised by my insider friends that I am a shoo-in. I am, therefore, devastated when the news breaks that I have missed out (again). For the record it has gone to some self-centered pseud called Andrew Motion.

My drive to bring The Arts and Business closer together is legendary. I thought my work as a poet would do the trick, with my acclaimed *Ode To A Restructuring Charge* and *I Love Thee Like An Unqualified Audit* landing me the Big Job. It was not to be, so I have moved to Plan B, and written a book.

My purpose here is not to plug the book (he lied), but to give you some idea of what's involved should you wish to do the same. Many of you will be confident you have a Big Idea; the one that will help millions of unenlightened business folk make sense of the zoo in which they work. It will also (purely as a by-product) make you rich and famous. You should be warned that it is a long and hard journey, and if you are successful you may have to have 20 extra teeth put in your mouth to look like Anthony Robbins. If you are not put off by that, here are the stages:

- First, you need a literary agent. The temptation here is to find a groovy, articulate, networking bookworm who will share the spirit of your work and join you in this literary mission. Forget that right away. You want a pit-bull. If it looks human it is a bonus. You need someone who worships St. Jude, the patron saint of lost causes. He or she will help you put together a Book Proposal, which some publishers will allow to be shorter than the actual book itself (but not many).

- Then you need a publisher, and what you need is one with a sense of humor. Thomas Harris has just released the sequel to *Silence Of The Lambs* after a wait of ten years. On the same day, at the same time I think, my publisher released my book. I believe this was to enable them to structure a 'fun' bet in their boardroom: that no book had hitherto ever been out-sold by eight million to one on its launch day.[14] It was either that or a barely disguised value judgment on me being the Hannibal Lecter of the business world.

- The book itself, of course, needs a Big Idea. I have to be care-ful here, because I understand that certain Chinese agents can access these pages, and I do not want to add to America's woes by giving them the secrets to our business success so soon after we have inadvertently given them the ability to bomb us into a black sticky paste.

---

14. It is very difficult to get actual sales data for book sales. The sales of my book might have been as high as 41, or as low as 37. I guess 39 is a good number.

I have, however, received CIA clearance to tell you that my book is based on two Big Ideas. The first will not be new to my regular reader: that there are not enough smiles left in the workplace, or in the literature relevant to it. I guarantee you will have some laughs if you read my book, unfortunately largely at my expense.

There are not enough smiles left in the workplace, or in the literature relevant to it

My second Big Idea is that we have made business too complicated. Life itself is governed by many simple, but universal, laws, such as death, gravity, and the fact that an American or Canadian team will win the 'World' Series in baseball. These laws govern all walks of life, from vacations (take half the clothes and twice the money) to buying wine (if the label has a picture on it, don't buy it). My thesis is that business, too, is governed by a series of similar universal laws: 101 of them. The book lists them for you.

Despite critical acclaim *('This author should be shot'—Charlton Heston),* I fear for my book's success, and may be forced into another dimension to link Business and The Arts. Movies will be next, and I am already working with James Cameron on another disaster movie to follow *Titanic.* It will tell a similar tale of a glorious launch, gilded decorations, stars everywhere, cheering crowds— and then a disastrous crash. Nobody saw it coming, thousands suffer, and it is impossible to experience it without weeping. Our working title is *Planet Hollywood.*[15]

---

15. Planet Hollywood filed for Chapter 11/Protection From Creditors in mid August. Ignore this column at your peril.

June 28th

Short Term, Me? Yeah, Baby!

• •

• • • IMHFO (In My Humble 'Rude Adjective' Opinion) the funniest stand-up comic alive is a guy called Eddie Izzard. He happens to be a family-friendly transvestite from Wales, so it's fair to say I can't be shocked easily. But I have to tell you, on returning to the US recently from a short trip, when I saw the billboards for the new Austin Powers movie *(The Spy Who Shagged Me)*, I fell off my horse.

A Federal ruling now forbids you to smoke, smile, or swear in any US business premises. So, for years, I have been getting away with a good curse now and again by using a few native English specials, including the 'S' word.[16] It may not upset you over here, but this I know: when my mother sees it outside the theater in England, she will attack somebody with her umbrella.

We remain, delightfully, two countries divided by a common language, and we're together in something else as well. Something scary. We are just about to enter into another season for corporate results, and I forecast they will be good. *Suspiciously* good. The economies of Japan, the old Soviet Union, Germany, the Asian 'Tigers,' and several big South American players have all given recent evidence of that circular, swirling activity recognized by all plumbers as the final movement before everything goes down the plughole. UK and US businesses should be in derived disarray, but they're not. And I smell heavy short-terming.

Short-terming a business to defend the next published earnings has been going on forever. The accountancy profession almost forces it: if you invest in an inanimate brick it is an asset—if you invest in a quality person it is an expense; if you invest in a fancy boardroom table it is an asset—if you invest in training it is an expense; buy a fancy jet, it's an asset—invest in brand equity, it's an expense. In addition, a determined CEO can drive a coach and horses through the loose international rules on audit, overstating revenues, and/or understating costs. Many companies live from one restructuring charge to another, and use them creatively to support earnings in between. None of this is new.

There are, however, a couple of new factors at play. Despite some inroads by minorities and women, the most common CEO profile in the US and UK today is of a white male in his 50s *with a zillion share options.* It is almost impossible to dream up a formula more guaranteed to short-term the business. Almost. There is one: a white male in his 50s with a zillion share options surrounded by a Board of his hand-picked cronies. Also with share options.

---

16. You can get away with murder if you know what you are doing and are confident. I once put my arm on the shoulder of a Burger King franchisee, smiled, and told him, confidently, that he was, without question, one of the greatest wankers I had ever met. He was ever so happy. I'll leave it to Austin Power's next movie to let the US in on the secret.

The most potent new factor, however, is one which we haven't begun to fathom yet, and it involves changes in investor behavior. Although the business world makes noises about recognizing varied 'stakeholders' in a company, in all honesty most Boards don't give a toss about anybody other than the financial shareholders. These are the people who buy and sell the company's stock, and thus largely determine its share price and total market capitalization. And it is these investors who are undergoing a structural change in their behavior.

A share transaction a few years ago was a thing of beauty. Although the big investors (e.g. pension funds) had their own specialists, most investors would buy and sell via a broker. It was a serious event. It was expensive in itself. The relevant information was limited, and there was an attitude that, even with genesis companies, it made sense to pick a stock and stay with it a while.

The implications for management are profound—you must look good *today*, or you are toast Today we have on-line trading, 24 hours a day across 24 time zones. There are almost infinite amounts of data, analyses, choices, and processes available to anybody who has access to a cheap PC and phone line. Many modern investors now switch whole, complex portfolios in hours, and do so every day. The implications for management are profound. You must look good *today*, or you are toast. Nothing else can matter.

Nearly 200 years after the event, Chou En-Lai was asked his views on the French Revolution. He replied, thoughtfully, that it was still too soon to judge. In the same way, it may be some time before this current paranoia and short-termism bites us back, but it will. And it will hurt.

Clearly this subject commands that I write another book. It appears, however, that there is simply no point in fighting this exciting new populism, so I shall call it *The Short Terming That Will Shag Us*.

July 12th

You Say Hello, I Say Goodbye

• •

• • • On March 2nd this year, the news broke like a thunderclap over my peaceful, 250,000 acre, free-range *escargot*[17] farm in South Miami. It was impossible to contain the elation, and I gave most of my workers half a day off. My chef and personal trainer were relieved until after luncheon. I decided to do without cufflinks for the morning.

For such celebations we would normally roast a manatee, but as they are now protected we made do with an enormous pink (male) tourist from Wisconsin.

---

17. Becoming *the* party idea of 1999.

The glorious news, of course, was the breaking story that Hewlett-Packard was 'de-merging,' spinning off its medical technology and electronic testing arms into a separate business, leaving the residue to focus on, er, 'computing.' The sexy strategy of combining measurement, computing, and communications was leaking oil. Two years of flat results were one thing, but more importantly for the company that spawned the *zeitgeist* of Silicon Valley, it had lost its technical leadership in the growth markets associated with its core competency. Sun Microsystems, Microsoft (with some *very* nimble footwork after nearly missing out on the Net), and even the revitalized Big Blue, all exploited HP's weakness in Internet servers and services—a weakness that came directly from being in too many businesses.

Barely 100 days after the March announcement, there is more good news and we roast another tourist, this time from Germany (which we serve with *fava* beans and a nice Chianti). With a new sense of focus, HP announces a powerful set of investments in the Net, and couple that with visions of technical developments in the fields of E-outsourcing and 'instant' on-line services. In only 100 days, this near-$50 billion company goes through a complete makeover. It may look cosmetic, and they still have to actually *do* it, but it took courage and conviction. I wouldn't bet against them.

They are not alone in this type of journey. Pepsi spun off its restaurant[18] brands (KFC, Taco Bell, and Pizza Hut), and in doing so backed two pieces of logic: first, that the restaurant businesses would be better run by people who had nothing else to worry about, and, second, that they would give Coca-Cola a better competitive fight if they could concentrate on it. Makes *big* sense.

The spirit of MTV's *Unplugged* is sweeping business The spirit of MTV's *Unplugged* is sweeping business. Of course, it won't be called *that*—it will need a name like 'strategic realignment' or 'paradigm shift'—but it's the same. I've grown up with a lot of rock stars from the get-go, and seen them evolve from tight, powerful acts to bloated, orchestrated, choreographed parodies. A three-minute video is a multi-million dollar production number, and a concert only counts if it can be seen from the

---

18. I use the word 'restaurant' in its loosest possible sense.

moon without binoculars. *Unplugged* provided an opportunity for many of these geezers to get back to their core competencies, and a few of them rediscovered what they were good at, and their careers entered into a new growth phase. Or, in Rod Stewart's case, he grew more chins.

Strangely enough, the same principles are behind a number of mega-mergers, although, on the surface, it would seem a trend in the *opposite* direction. In banking, for example, the threat from unconventional new entrants into the financial services market, together with the need to respond to massive technical developments (e.g. automated tellers and on-line banking) have meant that a totally new kind of corporate architecture is needed to survive and prosper in the core competency. That new architecture can be described in two words, *humun* and *gous*.

All this begs a question. If it makes sense to unplug, what's with McDonald's? Here you have a core competency behemoth, and one who has stuck with it. Shareholder rewards have been stellar. No unplugging is needed here. So why—*why*—have they suddenly decided to acquire a small branded Mexican food chain, and a similar gaggle of branded coffee shops in England? We can only surmise, but if their plan is to develop these into major brands in their own right, they are doing *exactly* the wrong thing. One way, and probably the only way, to risk McDonald's' future glory is to deflect capital, marketing, and management away from the core business. If, on the other hand, they have acquired these tiddlers as a cheap way of developing new products for their core brand, they are doing exactly the right thing.

I don't know. What do you think? Remember, this is the company who put seaweed in a hamburger (McLean) and launched that thing that looked like it fell off the MIR space station (McRib), so anything is possible. I wonder if they've thought of a German Tourist Burger?

July 26th
Live Like Flint

• •

• • • Noting the extraordinary sales of my new book, I asked the US Government's Office of Management & Budget to reforecast the outlook for my personal economics. They come back with the exciting news that my surplus is likely to be $1 trillion *more* than originally budgeted over the next 15 years.

I make a decision that I will use my new wealth to buy the town of Flint, Michigan, and to preserve it exactly as it was on Tuesday June 29th, 1999. That's the day the last General Motors car rolled off the assembly line in this, their corporate birthplace. Since 1906, almost 16 million cars have been made in this quintessential car-town. It was also a quintessential one-company town.

I picked this up in an international newspaper, and I mean no criticism of the *Miami Herald*, and the other US newspapers I surf, when I record that this event was noticeable only by its omission. I think I understand why. Unless you are among the collateral damage (i.e. you live and work in Flint), this information is just boring, a tad discomforting, and a long way away—and we all have much more exciting, comforting, and local stuff to write and read about.

We should, however, *all* pause and reflect on what's happened to Flint. It is wrong to think of it just as an untimely corporate mass murder and scorched-earth exit, and it is wrong that our emotions should just be grief and anger. Sure, we can 'blamestorm,' and take swipes at General Motors (motto: if all else fails, try management), intransigent labor unions (motto: we will argue with a sign-post), and unfairly favored 'foreign' car manufacturers, but the alchemy is more complex than that.

If you have never read Hegel, you shouldn't. He is the miserable, unreadable German philosopher, famous largely for inspiring Karl Marx and bequeathing the world about three sound bites. One of them (you don't want to know the others) is interesting when thinking of Flint: that *every idea contains the seeds of its opposite*. Maybe the death of a town contains the seeds of its life.

Every idea contains the seeds of its opposite

Had I been rich enough, I would have bought and preserved two other places: a little, dark, satanic, English mill-town called Mossley, and a country called Ireland. I spent early years of my life in Mossley, and 80 years before I was born it boasted the largest textile spinning factory in the world. By the time I arrived, war-fatigued Britain had lost its cotton markets and technology edge to India and Japan (yes, them already), and the town was dying. I drove through it again recently, and it had survived, but no longer as a blue-collar heartland. It is smaller, for sure. It has become a dormitory suburb of a nearby city. Its businesses are new, small, light, and service-sector oriented. But it is alive, and in shape for the next century.

Up to the mid-nineteenth century, Ireland's peasants depended on the potato as their staple food. This despite the fact that the island is surrounded by fish. I'm half Irish, so I have mixed emotions on all this, but the fact is the potato is a lazy crop. You plant it and sit around for few months, then eat it, store some, distill some into a fiery alcoholic drink, and then repeat the cycle. When the potato crop failed and famine kicked in, the English (that's my other half) landlords acted like tyrants and thousands starved. Thousands more fled to America and whined for the next 150 years. Just like Flint: an absolute disaster, with blame everywhere you looked. But you know what? Ireland has *never* depended on the potato since, and is now one of the miracle economies of modern Europe.

History has already clearly taught us that the one-company, one-business town is built on a San Andreas fault. It's not *if* disaster happens, it's *when*. Today, with a new twist of irony, the business or the company may not have to fail to trigger this. It might be the *opposite*, that to continue growth and *success* it may have to move production (or whatever) elsewhere. Such is globalism.

One way of beating disaster is to survive it, then stabilize, then come out of it looking better than when you went in. Mossley, Ireland, and countless others have done it, and I hope Flint does. It is better, however, to avoid it; and for all those still in a one-company, one-business community, there must be enough case history now to convince you to start spreading the risk *now*. Re-invent yourself before the apocalypse.

Buying Flint, of course, will still leave some of my new $1.0 trillion intact. I will call American Airlines and check the domestic US coach-class fares on a route where they don't have much competition. *That* should do it.

Momentary Insanity

• •

• • • Enough time has now passed to enable us to reflect objectively on the American women's soccer triumph. I am well qualified to do so, having loved and played soccer for nearly half a century. Manchester, my home city in England, has two professional teams: one is the most successful club side in the world; and the other is the one I support, thanks to my father. Their new motto (we came, we saw, we changed into shorts, we lost, we applauded the crowd) inspired my own playing career, which towered in its mediocrity.

The first thing *not* to do when reflecting on the women's success is to compare it with men's soccer. Trust me, just *don't*. Relax and celebrate the difference. By chance, the market value of Coca-Cola and America Online are about the same. It makes no sense to compare them, and deem one better than the other. They're both great, and both American. Enjoy.

Reflecting further: I spent thousands of hours in soccer locker rooms, and I can safely report that not one of those hours was spent in the company of anything that looked remotely like Mia Hamm. I should add, however, that many of my team mates over the years (particularly the later years) could have benefited enormously from one of those natty black sports bras displayed by Brandi Chastain when she put the winning goal in the Chinese onion-bag.

In more than 30 years in business, I have been a member of hundreds of business teams. I have had the privilege to lead many. The US women's soccer team reminded me of one aspect of effective team building which is just as important in the workplace as it is on any sports field: the need for the unsung hero and the workhorse. These very often come in the same body, as they did with Michelle Akers. The tendency is to focus on the high profile, media friendly, glamour-role specialist, but if you want the job done, most coaches (and business managers) will tell you that the first person written down on the team sheet each week is the unglamorous team-engine.

Dodge City (Inc.): I shall now turn my attention—seamlessly—to gun control. I was considering the implications for business of the recent Washington debate on the subject, where tighter controls were rejected. What really fascinated me was the counter proposal put forward, which was to pin up the Ten Commandments in the nation's schoolrooms. During my time as a Big Cheese in Big Business, I would make it my daily rule to break at least four Commandments by coffee time (although not always the same four), and I was pondering if the same dramatic counter-gesture could work in the boardroom. In mid-ponder, I came upon another gem: the governor of Louisiana has forced through legislation requiring public school students to call their teachers 'sir' or 'ma'am.' The details are hazy as to whether they are required to do this before they open fire.

Then it came to me where we've all been going wrong. About 20 years ago, I was appointed to my first real management position back in England. Like the immature plonker I was, I loved the instant elitism, which included all the worker-bees running around and calling me 'sir' and 'Mr. Gibbons.' Brilliant. Then one day I got into a long (beery) chat with my veteran sales manager. It transpired that, just before I was born, he had flown 19 successful Wellington bomber missions during the last years of the war with Germany, when air-crew life expectancy was normally about two such missions. He kept calling me 'sir.' It took me about a dozen beers to realize what I should have known long before: he was the 'sir' and I was the nobody. Three more beers and I took a decision that I have never felt the need to revisit: nobody should ever call me anything other than my ordinary name again—*however* fancy my official title. Sure, it is important to have respect as a leader, but, if you are lucky enough to be one, you get it through how the people you lead look at you, not through what they say.

It is important to have respect as a leader, but you get it through how the people you lead look at you, not through what they say

So, the answer to all Dodge City USA's maladies is to pin up the Ten Commandments in schools, and bring back deferential titles, is it? *Yeeeaah!* Of course. *That* should do it!

I have learned never to generalize about the wonderful, huge, diverse, US nation. So I offer the following with reticence. *You are wonderful* despite *your leadership.*

August 23rd
Decisions Required—
New Balls Please

• •

• • • Inspired by Hillary Clinton, I sometimes wander about Coconut Grove on a listening tour. Most 'ordinary' people I meet want me to talk about my legendary tennis career, which is surprising because it was so long ago. In fact, my last triumph was the 1917 Wimbledon Mixed Doubles,[19] when I partnered a young Janet Reno to a sparkling victory over a forgettable couple from Tibet. For the

---

19. The author may be confused here. As noted earlier, he also won the men's doubles with Fred Perry in the late 1930s.

record, it was the last major championship won using a whalebone racquet.

I still follow the game, and this year's Davis Cup has some interesting lessons for business. The Cup format is between nations, and two guys play an opposing two guys in four singles matches. There is also one doubles match, which often acts as a decider.

Earlier this year, the US team faced a difficult away tie against Great Britain. To make it harder, the two best US singles players, Sampras and Agassi, declined to play, so the team fielded two journeymen, Courier and Martin, in the singles. They won the tie, qualifying for the semi-finals against Australia, to be played in the US later in the year. Sampras then graciously decided he would be available for this.

This left the captain with a difficult decision. Do you stick with the loyal, patriotic guys who got you there? Or do you field the best side available, whatever the circumstances? For the fiftieth billion, trillion, gillion, quadrillionth time in the history of man, when faced with this kind of decision, the decision-maker fudged it. He picked Sampras, but only in the doubles. The result was a nightmare. Courier and Martin lost the first two singles. Sampras won the doubles, and the US went 1–2 down. They then tried to replace Martin, dubiously, by Sampras in the next day's singles, claiming the former's 'ill health.' The match referee rightly refused. Martin then showed how ill he really was by playing magnificently for five sets, but losing narrowly. Australia won the tie, and *everybody* in and around the US team was embarrassed and unhappy. Everything had gone wrong.

Fudging decisions is about trying to please too many people, and ending up pleasing none. And doing the wrong thing. It affects all walks of life. My home country, the UK, has been fudging a decision on Europe for three decades now, and shows no sign of weakening. We'll join the Common Market and NATO, but not the common currency. And we only want parts of EEC legislation. You see, we also want to try and keep our Special Relationship with the US (a relationship that, in truth, is as shallow as its current leaders). Oh,

Fudging decisions is about trying to please too many people, and ending up pleasing none

and there's also the old 'Empire' countries to placate. And we'd also like to secure our oil supplies independently. Fudge. Fudge.

Fudging is of epidemic proportions in business today. You have a salesman who has been running the east region, and has had a good year. But the circumstances were extraordinary, and he's probably peaked. Let's call him ... er ... Courier. Suddenly, central HR tell you of a superstar (who happens to be called ... er ... Sampras) who has been knocking them dead in the west region, and who would love to run the east. Do you put him in and break the first guy's heart, and feel awful? Or do you stay with him, and miss the opportunity to strengthen your team? Nine out of ten times, the decision will be fudged, and *both* will end up in the east—doing the wrong things for themselves and the business.

You own a small, declining, supermarket on a high street. Supermarkets are heading out of town, to huge buildings with acres of parking. The only things left on the high street are small, specialist, niche shops. Both of these options are too extreme for you, so you fudge and just try and do some *things differently*, instead of doing *different things*. Fudge, fudge, fudge.

There can be only one rule. You must be ruthless in making your decision. Ruthless. Zero-compromise. But once you've done that, you can afford to be *gentle in execution*. You cannot please everybody, so take the right decision, and then work on (and maybe invest in) managing the consequences.

So it is, today, with my tennis. It is now reduced to an occasional game with an Argentinian restaurateur (a possible oxymoron). With the full permission of our respective governments, we play for the stewardship of the Falkland Islands, or *Malvinas*, as he would have it. Let the record show that (as of going to press) the UK still have them. It is cheaper than war, and there are fewer deaths this way. But talk about fudging a decision.

September 6th
Here's My Year So Far. How's Yours?

• •

- I have been besieged by tabloid journalists after the news broke that George W. Bush and I briefly shared an apartment in Lubbock, Texas, nearly 30 years ago. They want the dirty on the guy. In fact, we lived there while we alternated shifts working the local Taco Bell drive-thru, and I didn't share much of his private life. I will admit, however, to some crazy parties. I will also admit to some wild moments, such as when, in a fit of anger at America's penal inheritance taxes, our future President took some of his family's proudest possessions (a glorious early period Renoir, and two Van Goghs) and cut them up into small pieces. I will admit he then ate all the pieces. But on the subject of illegal substances, my lips are sealed.

- I know what's behind the problems with Gillette. I have long been an admirer of this company's products. They are one of the few companies who do not rely on an 'our product sucks less' positioning in the market. This year saw the much anticipated launch of their *Mach III* razor, and although sales have been high, they may not have been enough to pay back on the rumored $1 billion development and marketing costs. That plus a few other scrambles and an earnings warning seems to have been enough to see their CEO depart a bit earlier than planned. My view? I think the *Mach III* may be *too good*. It cost 30–40% more than the Sensor, but I gave it a try. Brilliant. Next day I was in a rush, so I re-used the previous day's blade which I'd inadvertently left on the handle. Guess what? I got a perfect shave (readers please note: I do not have the need of some blue-beard guys to shave every three hours, so this may not work for all of you). The result? I spend the additional 30–40% cash, but have reduced units bought by 100%. I win, they lose. I wonder how much of this is going on?

- The world of golf this year is telling us something about what's happening in business leadership. Old generation management is characterized by Nick Faldo. He is old, white, miserable, past it, and whines like a saw-mill. If he ever wins a major again, I will climb the outside of Sears Tower *naked*, in winter, carrying only a low-fat latte. Behind him comes a young African-American, Tiger Woods—re-inventing the game and hugely media-savvy. An enormous gap in generations is evident in every aspect of how they go about their business ... but *wait*! Behind Tiger, *another* 'generation' is already making its presence felt in the shape of a 19-year-old *Latino*, Sergio Garcia. He is crazy and laughs and runs about and hits the ball miles. He makes 23-year-old Tiger look old and tired. Something exactly like this is happening with the people running business, and the only difference between me and Faldo as fellow-old-fogeys is I know I can be happy doing something else. It's not like we have a choice.

- I look at Starbucks stock price and fall into a dead faint. I am only revived by somebody dabbing Calvin Klein CK1 behind my ears, and loosening my undershorts. Howard, *stay off the Web*.

- The Oxford English Dictionary now contains the word 'greenwash.' We've got to know 'whitewash' quite well. In this century, we've had a much vaunted American President who was an acknowledged racist. We've had one of America's most celebrated entertainers who was an overt pederast. We've had a British Prime Minister run a *menage a trois* at No.10 Downing Street. There's nothing about any of them in the textbooks. That's whitewash. Greenwash moves on from that. It is a corporation pulling wool over everybody's eyes by claiming profit-friendly activities are actually environmentally friendly. My favorite is a sign in hotel bathrooms saying something like: *It's wrong for us to use the world's limited natural resources to wash all your towels every day if you don't need us to. Just leave the towels you've used in the bath, and we'll only wash them.* *Greenwash* guys! This is just a clever way of increasing operating margins. I'd have more faith if the money saved came back to me or towards getting new irrigation schemes in Ethiopia. Until they accompany such signs with such a gesture, I am putting the hotel industry on notice: whenever I see one I will not only use *every* towel, I will also dry my hair on the curtains and clean my shoes on the bed cover.

Greenwash is a corporation pulling wool over everybody's eyes by claiming profit-friendly activities are actually environmentally friendly

September 20th
I Was So Much
Older Then

• •

• • • Like most people over 50, I could bore for my country at the Olympics. It's brilliant.

I was chatting recently to a Bright Young Thing who was contemplating a career in business. Confidently sitting facing me, with a hard, young, body, just the lightest touch of lip gloss and minimal facial jewelry, it's fair to say I was impressed with what I saw. His name was Bill. His enthusiasm waned rapidly, however, as I launched into what I thought were helpful stories from the good ole days. How, when I joined Shell, in England, as a graduate in 1969, I was given a job as an Area Representative. That's with a capital 'R.' My dad thought I had won the lottery. It was a position of *mucho gravitas*, but as the new wave, we were very relieved to be told that we would be the first generation to carry out these duties without having to carry a hat and gloves.[20] By now Bill was asleep.

The truth is, those ole days weren't good. They were very different, and its sad to see things like the handshake cease to mean anything other than hello/goodbye, but much of what we say we miss, we shouldn't. On closer inspection, much of it was unhealthy.

I grew to hate the 'anniversaries.' Almost every week, it seemed, we would be called into the cafeteria after work and some poor Doris or Bert would be 'congratulated' on being with the company for 25, 30 or even 40 years. The would be given a token gift, which they had chosen from a range of three from a catalog in Personnel. They wore their best clothes, and had looked forward to the event for months, maybe years. The supervisor made a short, inane speech containing more cliches per square inch than a modern corporate annual report, and it was all over. I didn't see the movie until years later, and it was only then that I saw the likeness of all those Bills and Dorises to those corpses that kept walking up the hill in *The Night Of The Living Dead*. In hindsight, the latter were far more frightening. As Charles Handy described it (*The Empty Raincoat*: Random House), life for many people had three phases: *dependency, job, dependency*. And then, of course, you died.

Nobody—I repeat, nobody—joining a business today will do 40, 30, or 25 years with them. Few will do 10. The companies themselves will not stay in one form for that long. And the business world, and society in general, is a healthier place for it. Those days were not about the 'values' of security and loyalty. They existed because neither employee nor employer knew any different. Now both sides do, particularly those companies and employees starting out now. Lives—and careers—are fuller, richer, more changing, and more varied. Certainly some pressures are higher, and loyalty and security have come to mean different things, but we shouldn't mourn the passing of the cafeteria sessions for the Grateful Living Dead.

> **Nobody joining a business today will do 40, 30, or 25 years with them— few will do 10**

---

20. They would not have looked good with my 22-inch flared pants.

The *stupefying* boredom of those days also gets forgotten as we look back through the nostalgia lens. As post-war production turned from armaments to consumer goods, the science of the division of labor reached its zenith; boring, repetitive, manual jobs, week in, week out. The production line bred serious zombies. And there was little relief in the administrative side of the company. As corporations grew, so did the paperwork challenge, but until the microchip came along that simply meant more 'white-collar' clerks doing more repetitive tasks. Thousands upon thousands of people clocked in each day, and manually handled double-entry book-keeping, payroll, invoices, and accounts receivable: same building, same shift, same desk, same ledgers. And the same boss. These people were managed by a level of supervision whose sole qualification to 'manage' others was probably that they had, a few years previously, bombed Dresden into something that resembled grape jelly or incinerated vast numbers of Japanese.

That was not the Golden Age of Business. I'm not sure there's been one yet. Thankfully, the incredible march of technology, and the globalization of production has forced the US and UK to leave all that behind. Today, we're service and services oriented, with a lot of genesis companies. If you're good, there is a huge shortage of you. There is more opportunity than ever to marry what you want from a spell with a company, with what they want back from you. What's emerging *might* be a Golden Age. I would be hopelessy equipped to survive and prosper in it, but I am wondrously well-equipped to sit on the sidelines and bore everybody.

Did I ever tell you about my first monthy pay check? No? Weeeeell, let me tell you, sonny, today that would just about buy you a small Intel chip ... or a Big Mac. Frankly, they taste the same to me. Now in *my* day ... you could get a steak as big as Texas ... blah, blah ... just a few cents ... and as for *our* chips ... man, it took two horses to handle my first microprocessor ... and as for my walk to school each morning ... often in snow sixty feet high ...

13th October
I Don't Believe
What I Just Saw

• •

• • • They say you can't have a great rock band without a great drummer. But when Brian Epstein shaped the Beatles, he knew Ringo wasn't the best drummer in the world. Heck, he probably wasn't the best drummer *in The Beatles*. But he gave the band something that had been missing, and the whole imagery and awareness thing exploded. Sometimes you don't recognize great marketing for what it is.

Marketing, the maddening combination of science and art, has moved on as fast as any technology over the past 30 years. The new techniques for execution vary, with notable modern highlights including the most recent losing US Presidential candidate looking directly at a camera and talking very, *very*, seriously about something called *erectile dysfunction* on TV. An astonished generation of males suddenly realized that this symptom may *have nothing to do with beer*.

Although execution techniques have changed, and will change again (massively) with the advent of cyberspace, the basic goals of marketing remain the same. You aim to increase earnings (not revenues) by more than you spend in the attempt. Usually, companies recognize there are only three ways of doing that: attracting new customers; getting existing customers to buy more often; and getting all customers to spend more. That's where the consensus ends, in particular when it comes to the decision to target your efforts at potential new, or existing old, customers.

I once managed a beer sales and distribution business in England. Most of the pubs were tied for beer supplies to their brewery, but the big working men's clubs, with *huge* beer volumes, were independent and fair game for our sales team. When we reviewed a period's trading, we always found that we had won a few and lost a few accounts, but further analysis showed one competitor *never* lost an account once they had it. The company was run by a veteran beer man, and his goal (and method) was simple. Any rep who lost an account had to journey to Head Office to explain the circumstances to the Board of Directors, who would often convene just for this event. Ostensibly, that was for the Top Brass to 'understand' the market dynamics better, but the message got through to the field guys quickly: two or three such visits and a high correlation with your corporate mortality rate came into play. They would *do anything* to avoid one of these visits, so we faced competitors who would cheat, lie, steal, and (if necessary) kill women and children to avoid losing an account. Indirectly, this achieved the business goal of keeping existing customers, the idea being, of course, that it was far more effective and efficient to do this than chase new business converts with expensive discounts and deals.

Contrast that with BellSouth Mobility today here in Miami. I've been a cellular customer of their's for 10 years, and my old cellular carphone recently packed up. I decided to join the ranks of the carry-your-cellular-with-you-everywhere breed, and went for one of these deals where the mobile phone is on offer for a nominal cent if you buy the service. Fair enough. But I was then told by

BellSouth Mobility that this deal *was only for new customers.* E-x-c-u-s-e me? I'd been happily with them for 10 years, I wanted to stay, I needed to buy a new phone, and was prepared to sign a new deal. On hearing this exciting news, my existing supplier effectively told me that, to get a deal on a phone, I would have to sign up with a competitor. There may be logic in there, but it escapes me. If you stand close to whoever put that scheme together, you will hear the ocean. Trust me.

I know we live in the age of the virtually unsatisfiable customer, but that doesn't mean businesses should forget about loyalty—in both directions. Concentrating your efforts on your existing customer base is *by far* the cheapest way to achieve the goal of a bigger increase in earnings than it costs you to attempt to get it. Of course you need to generate awareness for your brand, and attract new customers, but to do so at the expense of securing the custom of those who do business with you now is foolhardy.

I know we live in the age of the virtually unsatisfiable customer, but that doesn't mean businesses should forget about loyalty

Of course, you might strike lucky in this marketing thing. It's risky to rely on luck, but it can be wondrously effective. The most successful US show ever on Korean TV was *Joanie Loves Chachi.* By the way, *Chachi* is Korean for the male genitals.

17th October

Here's The New Boss: Same As The Old Boss

• •

• • • Being a boss brings fascinating challenges. The first time I had supervisory responsibility was as a shift manager for a Shell oil distribution depot in England. I was very nervous as I took over from the day-shift guy, but he told me everything looked calm and peaceful. The only thing I had to watch out for was that a couple of contractors were coming in to do some maintenance on the inside of one of the huge, 4000-tonne oil storage tanks, which had been emptied in readiness. As there would still be a lot a lot of fumes present, it was traditional to give such contractors a credit note for a pint of milk each from the canteen. When this was drunk, it would, apparently, line their stomachs and prevent nausea. A tad Neanderthal, perhaps, but this was the 1970s.

They arrived, and, bless them, they were Irish. (I wish it wasn't so, because that makes this story a bit too near home, given my lineage.) I did as was instructed. I signed the note with my new executive flourish, and they got their cartons of milk. From my little office, I then watched with a quite surreal range of emotions as they slowly climbed the service ladders to the very top of this massive tank, crawled along the top and *emptied their cartons into the 4000-tonne void inside*. I had to write all this down in my first ever shift manager's log record: a document that you would have thought, given the intense hilarity it caused amongst my peers, had been written by *Monty Python's* scriptwriters. It was indeed a thoughtful young man who reflected on his first day in the executive world.

The fact is that basic one-to-one people management skills are still appalling, and, in my observation, worsening

It's not easy being a boss, and the challenge has toughened over the years as subordinates are more cocooned by regulation, and are more challenging and assertive in the way that society is in general. Control 'wingspans' (i.e. the number of subordinates reporting to one boss) have widened with cut-backs, downsizing and new technology, which means less time is available for one-to-one management, and *could* mean more healthy empowerment. In reality it has meant more bad interpersonal practices. The fact is that basic one-to-one people management skills are still appalling, and, in my observation, worsening. So I'm reduced to cynicism. Here's my charter to help *your* manager do a better job of bossing *you*. Address it to him/her, stick it in the inter-office mail, and wait for the response:

Barry's Helpful Hints For You To Give Your Boss:

- Never give me work in the morning. Always wait till 4:00 p.m. and then bring it to me. The challenge of a deadline is refreshing.

- If it's a really rush job, run in and interrupt me every 10 minutes to inquire how its going. That helps. Or even better, hover behind me, advising me all the time.

- Always leave without telling me where you are going. It gives me a chance to be creative when somebody asks where you are.

- Wait till my yearly review, and *then* tell me what my goals were. Give me just a cost of living increase. I'm not here for the money anyway.

- If you give me more than one job, don't tell me which is priority. I'm psychic.

- Do your best to keep me late. I *adore* this office, and have no other life.

- If a job I do pleases you, keep it a secret.

- If you don't like my work, tell everyone. I was born to be beaten.

- If you have special instructions, don't write them down. In fact, save them until the job is almost done.

- Never introduce me to the people you're with. I have no right to know. When you refer to them later, I'll try to figure it out myself.

And, finally, Barry's favorite:

- Tell me all your little problems. I especially like the story about having to pay so much tax on your bonus.